THE WRITER'S NOTEBOOK

THE WRITER'S NOTEBOOK

Edited by Howard Junker

HarperCollins*West*

A Division of HarperCollins*Publishers*

The prefaces and the notebooks of Kathy Acker, Sherman Alexie, Po Bronson, Ethan Canin, Karen Clark, Katherine Dunn, Charles Johnson, Maxine Hong Kingston, Martin Cruz Smith, Gary Snyder, Gerald Vizenor, and David Rains Wallace originally appeared in ZYZZYVA, 41 Sutter Street, Suite 1400, San Francisco, CA 94104, (415) 255-1282.

FIRST EDITION

Library of Congress Cataloging-in-Publication Data

The Writer's notebook / edited by Howard Junker. — 1st ed.
    p. cm.
    ISBN 0-06-258618-1 (pbk. : alk. paper)
    1. Notebooks—United States. 2. Authorship. I. Junker, Howard.
PN245.W75 1995
818'.540308—dc20

              94-42961
              CIP

95 96 97 98 99 ❖ RRD(H) 10 9 8 7 6 5 4 3 2 1

This edition is printed on acid-free paper that meets the American National Standards Institute Z39.48 Standard.

Contents

Introduction

> To ask for the whole thing cut and dried at once is a great error. There is no use sitting down waiting for clarity, believing that your work will reveal itself in a flash and show you the road to it free of charge. You have to grope your way in good faith and be content with little. In that way you keep your strength and courage alive.
>
> — Vilhelm Ekelund

*T*he "manuscript" has long been considered the most intimate evidence of the writer's hand—and mind—at work. But the handwritten *objet* was destined for extinction by the development of the typewriter in the late nineteenth century; Mark Twain is said to have been the first to create directly upon such a machine. And now, in the age of word processing, who knows how much "writing" disappears into electronic nowhere-land before a printout is even attempted.

To find the writer's hand these days, it is often necessary to step back to the stage before "creative" writing begins, back to the stage of "jotting down" in a writer's notebook. It is perhaps surprising how many writers still do "write" in notebooks, and I don't mean on mini-microcomputers but in little spiral-bound books with lined pages—or on napkins, scraps, what-have-you...

Using this primitive technology, the writer remains free to explore, to interrogate the world for whatever it might yield, whether or not the stuff discovered might later be subjected to aesthetic pressure. In a notebook, a writer can be uncertain, ungainly, unliterary. A notebook, after all, is only scribbling. It is not even homework, much less a term paper. The final exam still seems wonderfully far off.

1

The notebook is experimental writing in the best sense. Anything can be tried because nothing is at stake. No one is watching; there is no script, as there is in a rehearsal, to obey.

Even more than that most compendious literary form, the novel, the notebook is a catchall, such as a notebook Mark Twain kept in 1892, which D. M. McKeithan describes as

> . . . containing such miscellaneous items as railroad schedules, the names of merchants or locations of shops, reminders to himself to get tobacco, writing paper, or whiskey, a place where he could have Livy's watch repaired (near the Ponte Vecchio), a few dinner parties and the names of those present (sometimes with a few comments), letters or MSS sent to Fred Hall (manager of his publishing house,Charles L. Webster & Co.), names and addresses of people he had seen or would see or would write, comments on things he had seen in the Uffizi Art Gallery in Florence, and details and notes concerning *Pudd'nhead Wilson, Tom Sawyer Abroad,* and *Joan of Arc* while he was writing them.

Notebooks occupy a special niche among subliterary (or preliterary) genres. Like some letters, notebooks can be totally unstructured from line to line and can range in tone from businesslike to intimate. Like diaries, notebooks can reflect the first consciously attempted efforts to define a self. Like journals, notebooks can entail extended contemplation, often surveying a particular subject over time. And like scrapbooks, notebooks can function as grab bags, collections of images or quotables clipped directly from life, maintained for purposes to be named later.

Notebooks are, by definition, workbooks, deliberately kept as part of a transformative process: I take note of this now; at some later date I will refer to my notes, and they will help me summon up those aspects of experience I need to recall.

The notebooks of great artists—Leonardo, Klee—have long interested a larger public; notebooks of writers are much less widely appreciated. Recent attention to notebooks, however, has been inspired by French critics, who—having for decades insisted that the text is created by the reader, not the writer—are now shifting back to biographical/historical approaches, studying "genetic texts," that is, (rough) drafts and even notebooks.

I asked the American writer/critic Guy Davenport whose

notebooks he has read with pleasure. He was kind enough to respond in a long letter:

> Apollinaire, Matthew Arnold, Arnold Bennett, Samuel Butler, Vilhelm Ekelund (one of the great ones), Emerson, Victor Hugo, Henry James, Joseph Joubert, Kafka, Henry de Montherlant, Theodore Roethke, Wallace Stevens, Paul Valéry.... I suspect that the really interesting ones—Doughty's daily jottings in Arabia—are as yet unpub'd. Beinecke has a Pound diary, of which I've seen one page.... The subject is enormous: Practically all writers have some kind of first-draft workbook—Thomas Wolfe, Shelley, and you make me realize that the genre has many subdivisions. French writers keep thoughtful journaux—Camus, Gide, which are highly polished, and into this category we can place Lichtenberg's "trashbook" (Nietzsche's and Wittgenstein's favorite reading). The Goncourt journals are in effect notebooks as well as Hopkins's. Also: Drummond's ms book in which he recorded Ben Jonson's conversation during a visit, Scott's antarctic diary, naturalists' field records, the Lewis & Clark logs, Basho....

"The Writer's Notebook" is a regular feature in *ZYZZYVA,* a quarterly of West Coast writers and artists founded in 1985. We offer a selection of facsimile pages from the notebooks of well-known writers, with a brief statement by the writer describing how the notebook figures in the creative process.

Our notebooks are notoriously raw, uncooked sometimes to the point of illegibility. We've had to supply footnote translations for the most egregious practitioners of bad penmanship, Gerald Vizenor and Charles Johnson. Facsimile, nonetheless, seems essential to us, because even when only typeset, that is, minimally gussied up, a notebook entry becomes "writing," submits itself to evaluation as having been processed. So we take our chances. Notebooks, we feel, should remain as unadulterated by art—and editing—as possible. In their nakedness lies their charm. It is also attractive to us that they remain resistant to easy reading.

The first notebook came our way by accident. We had been after Martin Cruz Smith to knock out a short story for us, the way he used to do early in his career when he had had to hack them out for money. Over lunch one day he said that of course

he didn't write short stories anymore, but might we be interested in taking a look at something he had done as part of his research for *Polar Star*. He had done a one-night stint on a herring boat in San Francisco Bay and had come home to report his adventures in a notebook, in an elegant hand, interspersing his text with detailed sketches and meticulous diagrams. If we had had a suspicious nature, we would have thought that he had been working specifically for publication.

Our next notebook, however, erred in precisely the opposite direction. It was so crude, so inept, so desperate in its search: Kathy Acker uses her notebooks as a way-before-the-first-draft draft, struggling to achieve any clue at all as to what might eventually qualify as bona fide Kathy Acker.

As might be expected, writers are as idiosyncratic in the privacy of their notebooks as they are in the formal regalia of their published appearances. Gary Snyder keeps many kinds; ours is in the manner of a travel journal kept on a trek into the Australian outback. A few lines from this notebook actually found their way into a published poem. Maxine Hong Kingston keeps what amounts to a not-daily diary. Katherine Dunn jots down telephone numbers of sources for technical information she'll need to write scenes with authority. David Rains Wallace sketches the plants he observes in the Costa Rican rain forest because he knows he will want to identify them when he gets home to his library. Charles Johnson and Po Bronson take the classic approach, noting character tag lines, plot bites, chapter sequences. Dorianne Laux writes notes as part of the yoga of creation, in order that words might continue to appear on the page. And, as Karen Clark still waits for some perceptive editor to accept her first poem for publication, she continues the struggle in her notebooks.

I'm not sure I'd be willing to claim that our notebooks really shed light on the creative process, much less illuminate specific works. But they do provide necessary evidence that writing is a process, often an arduous, mysterious one. And that it is a process that can be followed along many different paths.

To writers, at every career stage, our notebooks offer, I think, a kind of ultimate, reverse inspiration: "Look how ordinary, how lost and styleless—and how courageous—a great writer can be. Just like me. Look how painstaking, how attentive, how committed to getting it down on the page a great writer can be. Just like I should be."

H. J.

KATHY ACKER

I now make five or six drafts for each chapter of my books. The last two drafts are typed, then read aloud, in that order, for purposes of editing. The earlier drafts consist of layers of material—other texts, dreams, bits of autobiography, thinking notes—which I delete rearrange add to and damage in each successive draft. The final draft of this chapter includes the dreams and little else as direct text; the other texts, such as the notes based on Jane Harrison's *Themis,* became indirect texts, narrational directives. I use black, blue, gray, and red ink on the right side of college-ruled, 150-sheet, 9½-by-6-inch, $3.59 notebooks.

I began writing with no precise goal, animated chiefly by a desire to forget the usual. recognizing the sex about whom you've also forever dreamt

FOLLOWING THE TRACKS OF DESIRE

THE LOSS OF MY HEAD

I'm going to find the witch? How? By telling tales—

Kathy Acker teaches at the San Francisco Art Institute. These are the first twenty-two pages (not including two blank pages) of the first of four notebooks she worked on while developing the "Dreaming Politics" chapter of her 1993 novel, My Mother: Demonology *(Pantheon).*

javān	جَوان	
hā zɛr	حاضِر	
bā	با	with
pā	پا	foot
tā	تا	(until)
yā	یا	or
āb	آبَ	water
bāb	باب	(gate)
bābā	بابا	papa
by	بی	(without)
āby	آبی	blue
jib	جیب	pocket
pich	پیچ	corner, screw, hoist
in	این	this
ān	آن	that

jā	جا	
injā	~~انجا~~ اینجا	here
ānjā	آبحا	there
biny	مینی	nose
Hāji	جاجی	pilgrim
beit	بِیت	verse
pei	یـَی	
bebin!	ببینـِ	see!
tab	تـَب	
bein	بـَین	
beyā bān	بیابان	
jān	جان	life
nān	نان	bread
tan	تان	
bayān	بَیان	

DREAM SEQUENCES - Bataille
as a woman on witches
war.
Because I'm beautiful even
effeminate, I loathe anything
that smacks of militarism.
all descriptions of men are sexual.
what does this deep-lying sex
mean?

at one point I'm at a crossroads.
I'm going to buy the dress that I
want. I've been at in this section of
the city in other dreams. Again, I
walk downhill (~~n~~ to where, in my
childhood, the bakery used to be).
At the bottom, not yet at the clothes'
store, I look down at my arms.
A worm has put its head to that
flesh. Then the worm enters. The head,
snake, is jutting out, unot yet breaking
the skin, in a gelatinous mass. I'm
appalled. I don't want these things
in me, eating me. I'll do anything
to get them out. I never want
them in me again.

In the 16th c. men thot that witches
were blacks cats & burnt them. The
cats have never forgotten ~~these~~
~~actions.~~ What men did to them.

...tracing the tracks of what is
(witches)

For everything sacred has the sub-
stance of dreams and memories.
So WE experience the miracle of
what is separated from us by time
(death) or space suddenly made
tangible.
What is the sacred? Horror? I.E.
the face of ex $ sight of death?
YES. (To go against life. TO SEE
the mind.)
So I am not on the tracks only of
desire... Ⓐ

I'm many stories up. Next floor I walk into sloping-floor huge round room, red carpet, same huge windows. Chairs in semi-circle around edge of room. Mrs. Ai(k)? has been giving her speech. She walks over to me, tells me how much she admires my work. A thin Chinese woman. I'm shocked. She's the one who started reading w/ me. Then a distinguished grey-haired female who's some media character shakes my hand & tells me my text was very interesting. The principal. I'm surprised. But I have to phone Buffalo to tell them what happened. Leave room. I have to get out of building by going down every floor. Back in my room, green carpet, a woman is going to help me, 3 rockers including Arlo show me what spoken records are now hip, I'll be able to get the plane out of here tomorrow. I begin to pack.

On plane. Have to climb over people to get to my seat. Over seats. Then my friend's elephant sits on my lap. Only a small animal? w/out skin. Leaves skin, fake fur on floor until last time when all of it tries to sit on me.

No, I don't want to write
always about the nightmare of being
w/ B.
~~what you don't want happening to~~ ✓
~~you.~~
~~These are the halls that shouldn't~~
~~be ventured.~~
~~I'm in the elevator that stinks of~~
~~piss, piss when a the bums rub~~
~~their cock head against walls because~~
~~everyone had to come. Sometimes I have~~
~~a cock head.~~ I write in secret.
~~I knew~~ Actually I know that I'm 2
people ~~& we~~ we are all writers. Because
I'm a writer. My No, I can't say
anything else now. If Orpheus ~~so learned~~
regarded Dionysius as his teacher,
why was he ~~killed~~ slaughtered by the
Maenads?
Something to do with death. Ⓗ
~~The I know that as soon as I leave~~
~~the elevator, I will have to go thru the~~
~~hallways of death. The elevator took~~
~~me to the topmost & I must have~~
~~me got travelled safely thru the~~
~~hall into the room that was to be~~
~~mine, but I don't remember.~~ Ⓗ
~~Inside my Inside my room was~~
~~unlike all that tay~~ I think that I
must have had protection to get thru
these halls. Sleeze & cheese.
This is a journey. I want to find out

What the journey business is about, dream. And I'll come thru w/ something, I who am & know nothing. (A)

My Sisters are witches. (A)

I can't be Orpheus because I'm not a male. (A)

I am blood & cunt the problem for any pagan is that there is no possibility of transcendence or escape: "He Must all things swing round again forever?"

The Orphic solution; engraved this solution in cypher on gold tablets tied around the necks of their beloved dead. Solution: to refuse to forget, to refuse to drink the Lethean waters (so repetition means addition, 'doing it new!') Drink only from Persephone's pool & so become an immortal lord of the Dead (?)

what's this about? (A)

I love fucking with him so much I can't think about any thing else. He fucks me to not only are all my brains gone but until I don't know how to do anything else but come & maybe something's

Ⓒ

happening to identity.
The Orphic mysteries? Ⓡ
Ⓡ spacious
I found myself in a ~~room~~ room that
~~was found, whose carpets were~~
~~red. This~~ I had found myself.
~~The bedrooms, The bedroom,~~
~~which was tiny, lay off just off~~
~~the main, was also found. The~~
~~room or this room was as gorgeous~~
~~as the what lay outside was~~
~~fetid, nasty, full of criminal.~~ Ⓡ
Ⓒ The streets were actually
smooth ~~malls open to the sky~~
outside malls. ~~Stores the~~ Open
counters, the new kinds of stores,
stood next to each other. I
walked down the smoothness,
looking for hair dye. I needed 2
kinds of solutions. When, at the
end, I found what I was looking.
for, I decided not to buy the
~~hair dye~~ bleach & color so that I
could wait. Ⓡ
See I'm a woman. It's men who
think I'm a negative cause I'm
crazy about fucking: I think
something positive. Something
about journeys I, blood, am a
journey.

15

MAKE PROGRAMMATIC: 1/2/3

Spread legs. Ⓐ
You see I'm already married
cause all we do is fuck when we
fuck This is how we fuck he puts
his cock in me we move a little
so that I get hot enough so my
cervix opens around him & then
kissed his head & while it's
kissing him, we just stay there
& fall asleep & when we
wake up, we're kissing. Ⓐ
There's more.

The Orphic solution is to refuse
to forget.
    Justine - she appears totally
sexual & then acts as if she's
ashamed, a virgin. The word
"fuck" for example, makes her
blush. ~~she not only the Hers~~
This shame not only makes her hide
her ravenous sexuality: her need to
be nothing makes her pretend, even
to herself, that she isn't intelligent.
Totally intelligent.
So hiding, she searches for the person
or event that can break her hiding-
let her come out- but she still
wants to be nothing now sexually. Ⓐ

Her mom ~~was~~ bossed men around.
Didn't want Justine. So tormented
Justine, made her catch a bad
skin disease. Justine saved herself
from this mother- mother hatred-
by throwing herself into intellectual
work. ⓐ
~~One of her~~ Men have not given her
what ~~she~~ wants which is impossible
so she's moving toward celibacy
& language. Her dad was weak
& once tried to rape her. ⓑ
This is J's dream: she's shock,
can't breath, in a car that jammed
between a woman-man and a
man-woman (her parents). A loud-
speaker announces her father's
become Chairman. After this dream,
J wants more from a man than
just sex.
(Why we don't want what WE
want —)

I WANT TO FIND THE SOURCE
OF DREAM.
WHY?
NO REASON.

~~Above my head~~ is the ~~apartment~~

~~of my sister & her new husband.~~

[~~Loss~~ losing my head: ②
  1) Santeria
  2) Sex — Cunt lips then cunt.
comes up. Takes over. Swoon.
  3) Swoon at beauty.

Oedipus lost his head.   ①
~~God~~

Finding myself again. I tell
him to go away. & then I tell him
to come back again.
I want this I want that I don't
want anything emotions run me)
crazy ~~I~~
~~I don't like this. I was calm~~
~~My sisters~~ insert of another dream:
~~I'm in a dee~~
~~In~~ my sister's room; ~~there's a~~ A
white bed leans against a grey
wall. Above this white bedcover
the numbers 13 & 22 are dancing.
First only these two numbers, then
all the numbers that are possible.
and sit on our bedspread. Ⓐ
My sister's bedroom sits on my
head. Ⓑ

END

※

The animals always know.
animals & dreams.

The bird eats the eye. (I)
(end of the dream)

SEARCH FOR THE MURDERER

at the end of the dream my eyes
are tired
getting the key away from
the flames.

It's not true. I'm not like
my mother. I'm not human.

All you animals. Go free.

(dreams are animals)

1) Women & death. Deluded women
who ride certain animals follow Diana
goddess of the pagans. Epona, a
mortuary divinity, w/ cornocopia
symbol of abundance. nocturnal
mistresses led by Abundia, spirits
dressed in white, in wood or stable,
where they let wax drip from.
their candles onto horses' manes.

SHERMAN ALEXIE

*M*y "notebook" is actually a U-Haul cardboard box where I toss every scrap of paper that I've ever touched with a pen, pencil, crayon, or typewriter: hotel stationery, paper, envelopes, etc. I fill these pages with poem ideas, rough drafts of rough drafts, story ideas, "great" themes I should be addressing, jokes, cartoons that become jokes in my reading routine (my secret wish is to be a stand-up comic), character sketches, outlines, random thoughts, grocery lists, phone numbers, and other stuff.

I like to play games with already-printed material: questionnaires, greeting cards, calendars, other people's letters. Newspaper articles, *TV Guide,* magazines, and such. I always try to surprise myself with these, look at language in new ways. All these things also serve as springboards for real poems and stories.

I keep the stuff I think is good really close to my writing station: a kitchen table. It sits in messy piles until I get the urge to look for something. I actually do a lot of writing in my head before I ever put any words on the page. But when I'm stuck, I'll just grab a random piece of paper and work with it. Sometimes I come up with something useful. Other times I don't come up with anything and just throw the paper back into the pile.

Eventually, those notes that I've worked to death (or that never worked at all) end up in that U-Haul box in my storage room. That's sort of like the Bermuda Triangle; nothing is ever seen again. But just like in the Bermuda Triangle, there are notes that do see the light again. The idea for my second novel, *The Custer Killer,* which I'm working on now, came from a note that had been lost for a couple of years in the U-Haul box.

Sherman Alexie lives in Seattle. His most recent book, The Lone Ranger and Tonto Fistfight in Heaven, *is now available from HarperPerennial. Grove-Atlantic will bring out his new novel,* Coyote Springs, *next spring.*

Airplane

Up here, where no Indian was ever meant to be
I carry small things to insure my safety:

~~the the~~ a book of short stories
by ~~the latest great American Writer~~
a ~~movie~~ magazine
a ~~feather~~
faith

Up here, where no Indian was ever meant to be
I carry the small and usual things:

a generic novel, movie magazine, a book of poems
by the latest great poet, and bottle of water, cool faith

or guilt, depending on the amount of turbulence
How did I get ~~this~~ to be this Catholic

and catholic.

D-Day Poem - Celebrating War just like Indians
and their warrior fixation so destructive
what to do?

Stephanie Inn

What
ever
an
ocean
smell
like?

Sex + death

Orgasm = little death - French?

The first time I danced
with my wife = dance

2740 S. Pacific · P. O. Box 219 · Cannon Beach, Oregon 97110

(503) 436-2221 · 1-800-633-3466

Father Terry died = flute - flute - flute

title?→

when I was my father
I sang love songs like this to ~~myself~~ me

World Cup Soccer = poem?

Why all the riots?
Why no riots in America?
    Answer: Soccer is boring
            I'd get pissed off, too
            Ayyy
    Answer: Money. The kind of people
            who need to riot can't
            afford to get in games!

Money, Money, Money

1) Call Tour Pach Crew People
2) Call Nancy re: Grou(Athletic Adrenne
3) which nights to stay in LA – Sat and Sun?
4) Call Bob-HL

To all the fuckers New Age

New Age New Age

I pray
that you live

long enough to attain
that particular brand of American fame

which allows you to become rich
without having to cause fear and pain

and that you once appear
on the covers of NEWSWEEK and TIME

Simultaneously, and then die
on the same day, I pray
that
~~should~~ the audience waited
to hear the news

that ~~some future~~ President
of the United States

has been assassinated

[marginal notes:]

O unnum
letty
to
do —
be want
fight back

A blade article

Men's movement

The Custer Killer
Novel idea:
Indian serial killer
of white men?

On the Golden Gate Bridge
Why I Am Afraid for the World

Because there is a NO U-TURN ALLOWED sign
on the Golden Gate Bridge

because there is somebody out there
who would attempt a U-turn

on the Golden Gate Bridge
and they need to be stopped

Jean Stewart — tell Bob I met her

traffic sign poems?

rush hour
Indian in a nice car
Cadillac Jack

do Indians jump
off bridges?

Bob's Coney Island

Let's begin with this: America.
I want it all back
now, acre by acre, tonight. I want
Some Indian to finally dance
the Ghost Dance right

Northeast
first day

Happy 6-Day
Job!

and send the white men back home
to wake up in their favorite European city.

I'm not cruel.

ugh! I'm not cruel cruel
cruel

Still, I hesitate
when Bob walks *us* around his Coney Island
{ the Cyclone
the skeleton of the Thunderbolt
the Freaks
the Parachute Drop

Did we
part
That
carnivals
are
always
sad.
They

which has not been used in 30 years
but still looks like we could tie a few ropes *on*
to the top
(why the hell not?)
and drop
slowly down ~~~~, spinning, unraveling

MONTH: _April 1992_

MON	TUES	WED
1 Wake up! Every story starts	**2** have lunch all day	**3** What day is it? It's Wednesday all day
8 Mt. St. Helens relapse	**9** after	**10** as a three p conk MT ST. HELENS
15 The IRS was founded by Cuati	**15**	**15** Pay Taxes →
20 Mick Jagger and Don Knotts	**21** My birthday	**22** My birthday
27 Kiss an Indian poet day	**28**	**29** Self-portrait in a convex mere

Refill No. 47028

THU	FRI	SAT/SUN
4 Call Reagan	**5** Coll Bush	**6** rest
		7 Sing Buddy Holly
11 do nothing as fast as you can	**12** recou +	**13** rest
		14 pray/prey
16 on the size of your dreams →	**17** and the value of your eyes!	**18** rest
		19 rest
23 My birthday your birthday too	**24** The Indian horses screamed! *	**25** (un)rest
		26 church
30 I've kept one of those promises I was supposed to keep	**31** so I can travel those miles and sleep and sleep	**32** movie
		33 more church

© 1992 The Mead Corporation

Refill No. 47028

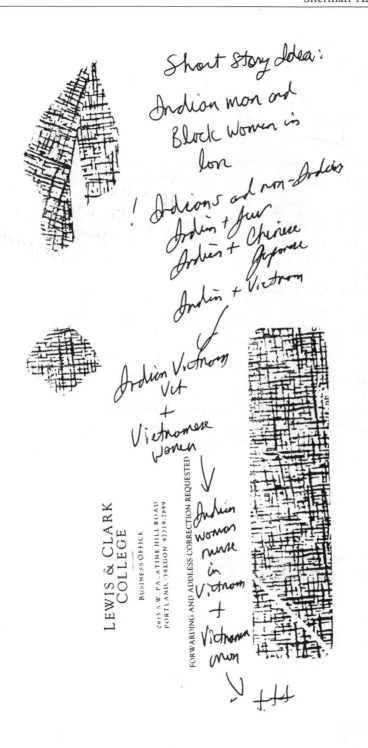

YOUR THOUGHTS ARE IMPORTANT!!

"Many Visions, Many Voices"
EVALUATION
Please place on the registration table before you leave.

What were your goals or expectations before you came to this conference?

My grandmother died of cancer, but before she died, a thousand Indians came to see her. We have evidence, the thousand photographs of P.) Mom and her current mourners.

Did the workshops and focus groups meet your needs?

· The Indian boys on my reg are spraying lysol on Wonder Bread and eating it.

What did you like best about the conference?

There were ghosts in my hotel room, but they were boring

What could be improved?

and didn't know any stories I hadn't heard before

What kinds of literary events would you like the Network to hold in the future?
Where would you like them to be held?

I want to go to a powwow Diane says she misses the powwows. I wish I was a dancer.

Do you subscribe to a North Carolina Literary Magazine? If so, which ones?

The Holy Bible

Other comments.

Nobody loves nobody and I don't even like my shoes.

Thank you for taking the time to answer this evaluation. Your input helps us as we design new programs.

found poem!? – epigraph! – short story! – essay!

Longstanding Claim Finally Settled

BOULDER, CO — An intensive 18-year legal battle by the Native American Rights Fund ended last fall with a land claim settlement for the Catawba Indian Tribe of South Carolina. The large settlement attempts to right a 153-year-old wrong.

The bill (H.R. 2399) provides a settlement worth $80-$90 million, including $50 million in cash ($32 million from the federal government and $18 million in state and local contributions) over five years.

The settlement also restores the tribe's federal status and trust relationship that Congress terminated in 1959.

The funds will be used for tribal land acquisition, economic development, social services and elderly assistance, education and per capita payments to tribal members. In return, the tribe relinquishes its claim to 144,000 acres, 15 miles south of Charlotte, North Carolina.

Gilbert Blue, Chief of the Catawba Tribes expressed relief that the long legal battle was over:

"We believe it is a positive resolution that will benefit the tribe and the region," he said.

Residents of York and Lancaster Counties also probably breathed a lot easier. If the legislation had not been enacted when it was, the tribe was poised to sue individually the 62,000 "landowners" of the contested acreage.

The claim dates back to 1840, when the state of South Carolina took the Catawbas' 144,000-acre reservation in violation of federal law and gave the land to settlers.

Negotiators from the tribe, from federal and state governments and from the locality worked out the agreement.

The Native American Rights Fund is a nonprofit Indian legal organization representing Native American tribes and villages, groups and individuals throughout the Unites States.

NARF can be reached by mail at 1506 Broadway; Boulder, CO 80302. Their phone is 1-303-447-8760.

grandmothers varg

As Nancy Lowley and Cecile Abrahamson eye the cake, Kimmy Brisbois sneaks her great-grandma Catherine Andrews a hug at a February dinner. The dual-purpose dinner recalled Mrs. Andrews 81st birthday January 28th and served as a baby shower for Trevor Heath (another of Mrs. Andrews' many great-grandchildren).

Indian Health Studies Injury Deaths

(Washington, DC) — A new Indian Health Service study may help further reduce fatal injuries among American Indians and Alaska Natives.

The *Injury Mortality Atlas of IHS Areas, 1979-87* was published last December by the National Centers for Disease Control. In the atlas, CDC examines common injury deaths among Indian Health Service clients in the 12 IHS service areas around the country.

Richard J. Smith III, the manager of the Indian Health Injury Prevention Program, commented that the study should help tribes become more aware of injury deaths and encourage them to develop new prevention programs.

The eight most common fatal injuries identified by the study involve firearms, falls, motor vehicles, homicide, suicide, drowning, poisoning, fires and burns. The deaths are categorized by sex and age of the victims and are compared to other U.S. racial groups. Up to 1981, injuries were the leading cause of deaths among Indians and Alaska Natives.

↓ poem ↑   *chant*

Writing Congress is "No-No" for Tribal Staff

The Spokane Tribal Council has ordered its staff not to write to Congress without approval.

The memorandum on tribal stationary and posted at the Wellpinit BIA reads:

> *Memorandum*
> *January 31, 1994*
> *TO: All Staff*
> *FROM: Tribal Council*
> *SUBJECT: Congressional Communications*
>
> *Please be advised that the Spokane Tribal Council must approve of all direct communication with Congressional Leaders and their staffs. If you need to address specific tribal concerns with Congress please present these issues to a Council member prior to Congressional contact. The Tribal Council requires this be done to ensure that all statements made on behalf of the tirbe are correct and represent-*

ing the true position of the Spokane Tribe. If you wish to discuss this memo further please contact me at your convenience.

P.O. Box 100 Wellpinit WA 99040
(509)258-4581/838-3465

Instead of an individual name the memo bears the initials: B.W., W.S., J.F.S., J.K. and C.S. The five Tribal Councilmen are Bruce Wynne, Warren Seyler, Jim SiJohn,

John Kieffer and Chuck Samuels.

The memo also includes the notation that copies had been sent to Land Ops, G.A. Credit & Forestry (apparently BIA Land Operations, BIA General Assistance, Tribal Credit and BIA Forestry).

Watchdog

DOROTHY ALLISON

*T*he last time we moved, I stashed most of my journals in a couple of cardboard boxes, planning that I would put them up on shelves in my office when I got the time. Almost twenty years of books are now jumbled together in no particular order. Only the last year's books are organized, over near my desk. The rest are shoved out of the way until I need to check something.

I did not go back the full twenty years to find some pages to publish. Some sections are very hard to re-read, particularly the year before I left New York, when I was continually sick and depressed, and the months after my mother's death. Some I just could not face right now, don't have time or emotional energy to spare. Shuffling through the books makes me think about why I keep them. It's not just the recording of facts but the place where I put a lot of my hopes and fears. The writer's life is so oddly splintered/isolated and internal most of the time, with moments of intense self-exposure. I think of the journal as a witness, a repository and playground. It is where I begin things or bring thoughts to some kind of clarity.

I have been typing my journals onto computer and then printing copy, which I insert into bound books, since 1985. In early 1993, I realized that it was silly to keep dumping the files after printing them out. So my journal exists in two formats: computer disks organized into a series of files by year and Cadic notebooks with both handwritten and computer pages inserted.

Dorothy Allison lives in Guerneville, CA. Her novel Bastard Out of Carolina *(Plume Contemporary) was a finalist for the 1992 National Book Award for Fiction. She is also the winner of two Lambda Literary Awards for* Trash *(Firebrand Books). Her most recent collection is* Skin: Talking About Sex, Class, and Literature *(Firebrand Books).*

The computer files are handy. I can check back for specific dates or names—a college where I did a speaking engagement, or a magazine, or an editor. Except for the occasional assistance of a young woman who helps me answer mail a couple of days a month, I answer quite a volume of mail and telephone requests that I can't refer to my agent. I try to keep that work to one or two days a week. The computer helps, particularly those evil but necessary form letters.

I use Cadic notebooks, which come in red, black, and gray. I used to try to alternate the colors, but forgot too often. Now I grab whatever is on my shelf. I buy these books in art supply stores where the cost varies tremendously. I have paid as little as $4.50 for one and as much as $12.00—that was when I had to buy one at a little stationery store in Atlanta. Usually I buy half a dozen at a time to get a volume discount. I tend to use three or four a year. The book is 7½ by 10, so it fits in a bag easily. It also has a fold-over flap that I can use as a place marker and a pocket in the back where I can tuck things, a calendar or notes or photos. I put in my hard copy from the computer file or do handwritten entries as I choose. I used to tape the pages in, but now I staple them. I found that the tape dried out and fell off, turning the journal into a pile of loose pages and clippings.

I keep a lot of clippings in my journals. The clippings range from two-sentence notes I pull out of magazine articles, letters, and news reports to photos from various sources and even horoscopes clipped out of magazines. I used to set myself exercises, such as doing short stories based on fashion photos, but I haven't had time to do that in a couple of years.

I do handwritten first drafts of both stories and essays in my journals. That makes them fairly easy for me to locate by flipping through the book, but I also sometimes stick Post-its on the pages where I have been working on unfinished stories. I tend to begin stories either with people talking to each other, or with narrative poetry—lyrics that get stuck in my head. I only start typing into the computer when I go to second draft. I do this partly because my eyesight has become so much of a problem that I avoid looking into computer screens, and partly because I like the look of the handwritten paragraph on the page. However, few people, other than my lover, can read all of my handwriting. Sometimes even I lose a few words. Then I have to make up something else.

Twenty years ago I used to keep two or three notebooks at the same time—one for a journal, one for fiction, and another for meetings or classes. That became too cumbersome. It seemed that whatever notebook I did not have with me was the one I always needed. And carrying them all around was hard on my back. I did go through a phase of writing song lyrics in a beautiful book of handmade paper I was given, but that book was lost, and I got superstitious about doing special books. For a long time I had a rule about using only one journal/notebook at a time. That changed with *Cavedweller,* the novel I am working on now. It has been written almost entirely by hand in two notebooks that I picked up several years ago. I wasn't sure what they were for when I bought them at a sale of discontinued stationery, but I had to have them. Both have a clean, wide-open feel with distinct black lines and hard black covers, ringbound so that I can fold the pages back and lay the paper flat. The heavy black lines also feel very sexy and kind to my eyes. I thought I would use them to start writing some poetry again. I didn't know they were for *Cavedweller*—for Cissy and Clint and Delia and Randall. But one morning I woke up very early hearing Cissy telling me how much she hated Delia for taking her back to Georgia, and I started writing her out in one of those black notebooks. A couple of months later Randall and Bugger took over the other one, telling their version of picking Delia up in the rain one night in 1973. Bugger took over the second book and now I have his whole story separate. I think he wants his own novel, and I wish I had half a dozen more of those black-lined notebooks. My eyes love the lines. My hands love the paper.

When a first draft is nearly complete, I start assembling the pages into a book shape—a notebook with chapter dividers or character sections. That's where most of the work takes place— long careful rewriting to get the seamless story I want. That's when I go back and forth from the typed copy to the handwritten notebooks. I got to that point with *Cavedweller* this summer after I set Bugger aside and promised him his own novel. I started typing the whole draft onto the computer furiously during the days, while still working by hand in the notebooks in the evening. I thought for a while that realizing I was telling two stories kicked me over into completing the first draft, but I think another factor was discovering that a box of my files and parts of some of my

journals had been soaked when a waterpipe leaked during the last earthquake. I had a shocking thought that the whole story—all those long nights of people talking to me—could be obliterated by one unlucky glass of Coke or cup of coffee. I've been typing and copying pretty furiously ever since.

My Cadic books are not beautiful, not special looking, just practical. They are nothing anyone would find too interesting. Part of why I chose them is a consciousness of what people pick up. In twenty years I have had two journals disappear: one taken by a girlfriend who gave it back to me after a few days and another that has never turned up. That book—from May through November 1987—was written before I started keeping computer files, so it is gone completely. It feels odd to have lost it and any record of that time—the period in which I made the decision to move to San Francisco and then moved. Worse, though, was the theft of the manuscript notebook of *Bastard Out of Carolina,* which was stolen—along with the rest of my luggage—in Los Angeles in December 1990. That was the month after my mother died and there were about sixty pages in that book that existed nowhere else.

I still remember the way I felt—standing out in the street in front of A Different Light Bookstore with Bo Huston. It was his car that had been smashed and robbed.

Bo said, "You have a copy, right?"

I said, "Not of all of it." And I just looked at him.

I had this overwhelming feeling of shock, despair, and odd exhilaration. I thought, I could quit. I don't have to finish this book. It was an astonishingly attractive idea. Hours later, though, staying over at Bob Flanagan's place, I woke up shaking. It was two in the morning, and the shaking didn't stop until I found the Cadic journal in my handbag—the only bag that hadn't been stolen. I started writing furiously, turning life into a kind of novel. That is what I use my journals for, perspective and madness, a tool to save my own life. It works for me.

We do not know how to die
but they teach us

We do not know how to live
but we make do

August 27, 1990

The Boundary between her body and
mine is a thin skim of sweat.

light sheen of liquid

Diffusion

Her breath, mine, mingling

Wind coming up.

My toes curl, nipples harden
labia protrude, tongue swells

The wire of my soul
lower chakra to highest
pulls

I can hear/feel/smell her blood heat.
her pulse

Her eyes open
mine close
Rivers in other states leave their banks, wander
Everything green trembles.
Rock heats.
there are volcanos, earthquakes
sudden tides.

Her thighs part
mine thrust.

Wednesday   June 6th

Well, I've lost my keys and the phone is broken. Can't go anywhere or call anyone. Kind of a relief.

Thursday   May 7, 1990

Got the epigram for Bastard...

"In the private chambers of the soul, the guilty party is identified, and the accusing finger there is not legend, but consequence, not fantasy but the truth. People pay for what they do, and still more, for what they have allowed themselves to become. And they pay for it simply: by the lives they lead."
                                                    James Baldwin

Finally back from Los Vegas, it feels like, though we actually got here Monday night. Too tired to think then, and Tuesday there was so much stuff...Sherry Glazer to talk to, Joy, Jeff with no good news about NAL, and my class to run that night. Just barely got everybody's stories critiqued. Then yesterday was just a lost day, still coming back partly, but also the phone was broken and I had lost my keys.

For Bastard ——

Elyse talks about Karma the way my Aunt Alma used to talk about Jesus. Good Karma, state of grace. Bad Karma; you've got Karmic debt, the stain of Jesus' blood on your soul. I've been washed in the blood of the lamb, but my soul is stained, stained black. Maybe I'm carrying a debt from an earlier life? My debts are big enough, I think. Blood and murder, a rebellious soul, lust even.

I'm not a good person, I tell Elyse, wasn't born to be.

She gets out her cards and tells my fortune. The hanged man, the Fool, the Five of pentacles, Four Kings.

"That's rare." "All Fours!" Her long hair with the little braids falls forward across her gray eyes, she tucks it all behind her ears, stares down at the cards and starts to rub her thumb across her swollen lower lip. The bruises under her left eye are grey-blue, stark on her pale skin. She'd be a beauty if it wasn't for her nose; says when she's "grown and gone" she's gonna get it fixed. She marry herself some rich old man.

"Karma," she nods. "You got just a lot of stuff going on." She tucks her thumb and forefinger and walks them across the cards like a —— laying out an ace

Saturday
June 30, 1990

Sitting in my rocking chair, working on the new LTE. Feels strange, casual, luxurious, indulgent. Quite wonderful in one way, like pulling over a notebook and just writing...not at all like booting up the computer. That big solid thing. This is tiny, to hand, like my own thought processes. Makes me feel almost like a free person, not tied down to the vast array of material things around me. Pity the battery only really *been* lasts three hours. But I suspect they will make them better as time goes on and I suspect I will buy them.

Had E̶l̶l̶y̶ B̶u̶l̶k̶i̶n̶ here last night to sleep over so she could give the people she is staying with a break. I was not in much shape for talking to her...have not been sleeping. Just about an hour a night for the past few nights. I go to sleep for about an hour...just til the first exhaustion wears off and then I wake up suddenly—anxious, trembly and with my head going at full speed. I think about my book, about money fears, BK, Alix, my mama, all my aunts, the way the world goes, Jeff and how reliable he is and is not. I think about this book of essays I am to write and what after all I truly know, what ignorances I will be exposing and subjecting to the world's criticism. It will mean talking to people like E̶l̶l̶y̶ again, critical, sharp-minded and impatient people. Can I deal?

Mama is still sick, but has not called to tell me the results of her biopsy. I suspect she is just delaying calling me. May not have the results back yet, and then again may not want to tell me—bad news or uncertain news. It sounds like she is weak, tired, a little depressed and a lot angry. Anger is the fuel of ulcers, the burning inside. Mama never admits how angry she is, just as I don't. We are the same creature sometimes. Too much so.

And CANCER. I expect to die of breast cancer. Yes. And that is one thing I have been thinking about these nights when I can not sleep. I expect it, and hate it, and rage against my own helplessness. Barbara told me about Cousin Billy dying (while Cousin Bobby with her home and equity, and insurance is doing well though they were diagnosed within the same month)—how her daughters stole her morphine and and Bobby and Patsy had to move her to a motel to die. Dead in three weeks, five from diagnosis. So fast and so horrible. Still Mama tried to reassure me, said "it was an easy death" meaning I guess that she was not in such terrible pain. Physical pain, Mama meant. I imagine Billy lying in that motel bed, swimming in morphine and time, looking back over her life with that comforting drug confusion softening everything. But it could not fix it, could not make it better than it was, only numb pain, grief and anger. What in the end would she have been thinking? Remembering the children that welfare took away from her? Or the men who left her? Or her sisters who always did better than she? Or her children who treated her so badly in the end? What does her life come down to? Her children? The only thing she leaves behind. Oh I would rage. I would spill bile down the ages.

Friday   July 6, 1990

Alix has gone off to camp out with Dee & DK, and Dee's sister
Darlene and her boyfriend. I am staying home to get some work done,
feeling bad about the fact that she is the only one up there without
her lover. But at least we talked about this problem before she left.
Both of us agree that this stint will just have to be worked through
but we are just going to have to move to a place that has a room where
I can put my office and close it off. She hates feeling like her
being here interferes with my work, and I hate feeling that I am
chasing her away when I have to work. But I also hate feeling that I
need her to be out of here, or for me to go away to get this book
written.

But much of this comes from my bad work habits. All of our
mutual fears and uneasiness are partly a product of my own avoidance.
It is not Alix that prevents me from working; I am my own problem.

Well anyway, I got the Winterson review done and off to DC by fax.
Came home to a message from Jane Troxell thanking me for getting it to
them. Also a message from Sarah Pettit at OUTWEEK, asking me if I
would like to contribute to a censorship issue they're doing at the end
of July (!). She'll call back early next week to check in, certianly
sounded like she wanted to chat. She also said she had gotten a phone
call from the Penguin Publicist asking her if they had a pictue of me
for publicity purposes. That's just how things are gong in the mad
mad world of New York publishing.

I need to call Nancy or get that letter off to her, in order to
get some cash to hand. Don't know when the house money will come
through, could easily carry over forever, or until we go to court in
October. And the N.A.L. money may not come through til October or
November, if then. Nothing is predictable, except a few royalties,
some money from the British rights to TRASH, and teaching—the gig at
SF Art Institute and whatever I get from teaching another class at
Different Light. Both of those require some prep work which I can't
get to for a while.

Joy called this morning; coming in Tuesday, July 17th at 12:55
and leaving that Sunday night. Wants to lie on the couch while I work
at BASTARD. Don't know if that will work. But can't think about that
right now. Have to chekc on this trip to L.A.—just how it is to be
organized and paid for. Don't want to do it but don't see any choice.
Got a letter from Gayle Suber today, the new Different Light reading
coordinator, asking if I wnt to set up a reading 1992. How can I
think that far off? Have to though, just like all those other
writers.

My earliest memories are of my
Aunt Alma's house where she lived out
near the Eustis highway, back behind the
little store she and her husband were trying
to manage. She had already had both
her sets of twins, the girls and the boys
and little Butch was a toddler with fat
sticky hands and enormous brown eyes.
I remember us all on her porch in the
early evening when the heat had begun to
slack off and twilight made everything
soft and magical. The boys sat with
their legs dangling off the side of the porch
waiting for the first fireflies to appear.

metallic aching echo of a slide guitar
rippled softly from the radio in the kitchen,
and the girls were bent over a washtub
of snapbeans that Granny was picking
through. Granny was pulling them over
their fine gir't fingers, through the beans
while she leaned back, tilting her cane
back chair so that it rocked on the
back legs. She kept rubbing her neck
and looking over toward the sound of the
highway traffic.

I hung behind her against the
wall next to the kitchen's screen door,
listening to the whine of that guitar, the boys'
thumping kicks against the side of the porch

We lived for a while in a sea of grass a little over and down from the Rhythm Ranch where neighbors set far enough away that you could barely hear their radios during the day. The grass was taller than a child, almost as tall as a man, full of thrashing sibillant creatures, snakes, lizards, chickens and frogs. Spiders and big water bug crickets. Most would flee if you stomped hard enough though pushing the grass ahead of you so that it lay down. Or you could sidle through leaving only a slight ripple and be invisible in an acre of yellow-green. Go far out into the middle and lie down so that you woke up through stalks reclining in a pushed down pallet. Safe, hidden. Only the far off radios held you to the conscious world, reminded you that sooner or later you'd have to crawl out, scratching red weals of bug bites and the pink stain of sunburn.

My sister does not remember her childhood. "She reads my stuff," she tells me, "in order to see what it was like." "But I write fiction," I tell her, even when I am writing about childhood, it is never the only story I am telling. "OK" she says, "But the childhood they tell us we survived isn't the only story either."

I think about that, knowing she's right but also grieving what is lost, what is unknown the memories I do not have and if I did have them would I want them? Those grains in mama's snapshots where my eyes are all enormous and empty? At any moment the story I am telling is only the story I can tell right now — the one I have gotten to the one I almost understand. I know there are stories I haven't yet imagined, haven't yet pieced out or understood how to tell. And those stories are dangerous, not only to those who will read them or misread them not understanding what fiction really is, but also dangerous to me, terrifying and painful for what I will have to know about myself in order to write them. It's as I tell my students over and over, you don't have to be a good person to write well but you do have to be courageous.

Wednesday Thursday   <u>May 18, 1993</u>

My hip is extremely sore, ache all over. Quite amazing how suddenly and
horribly your life can be changed. I could have killed myself, broke my neck or my
leg, fucked myself up so badly I could not have worked for a long time. And my heath
insurance still isn't in effect. But hell, my plane could have gone down any time in all
these months of travel, car crash, heart attack, anything. Life is what you ignore until
it is threatened. This life I have fallen into, worked at, and discovered is a continual
astonishment. Don't feel in control of it. Mostly I am in awe of everything that has
happened. Not that I have not worked to be this person, but I am still convinced that
the determining factor is mostly luck...or magic.

I have moments when I think I dreamed my life into existence.

But I am happy. Looking over at Alix standing in the kitchen doorway, framed
by all the bright and dark patterns of green trees, smiling and relaxed, I felt it move
through me like sex. Surprised me yesterday when Blanche was interviewing me for
the Nation and asked me if I was happy. Had to say that I was uncertain about saying
it but that yes, I was. Same as at the BABRA awards ceremony when it surprised me
so to hear myself say that I was happy. But suddenly sort of secure--money, worth,
work--and love, great love for Alix and Wolf that comes back to me in such powerful
measure. Extraordinary. I look into Alix's face and am astonished by the way she
beams at me and the way she makes me feel.

Is this the point? *Is this what everybody else knew that I didn't?* The way that
life changes around you and you discover yourself happy for long moments. Thank
you god.

I need exercise, both to get my weight under control and to work on my
depression. It might even help me with the writing. So much I need to do, be doing.
Yes, it is true that Wolf takes up enormous amounts of energy and time. But he is also
a source of belief, love and meaning. Right now he is lying on the bed with me, his
little hands curled up, his cheeks all pink, his smooth skin pearly and shining, and his
eyes partially opened while he sleeps. My hearts swells with love when I look at him,
the way he pulses for Alix. He is on loan to us, Alix told me, not really ours, only
guesting with us. Of course, and he may be a major pain in the butt as a teenager,
foolish, self-destructive, heart-breaking or even frightening. But he is a promise, an
act of faith, and right now a great bursting well of love. His love for us is as great as
his need, and more wonderful. Now he's jumped into a new stage, more brain cells we
tease, sudden increase in coordination and perception. Clearly he is pretty damn
bright, figuring us out swiftly and manipulating us as deliberately as he can, baby-style,
now toddler style. No evil in him, just want. He climbs, crawls, hangs onto our jeans
with one hand and rocks in the air, wanting to walk as we do, go places, do things.
My my.

3 PM.   Junior is fairly settled, finally asleep
after hours of crying every time I step
away from them. I am tired, restless,
eager to get home. Feel like I'll never
catch up on all my work.

I was a quiet baby, my grandmother
told me scarey quiet with big eyes and
two fingers tucked in my mouth

Amy Bloom

Windsong Music   Old Redwood Hiway   (otat.

The rain surrounded the cabin . . . with a whole world of
meaning, of secrecy, of silence, of rumor. Think of it: all
that speech pouring down, selling nothing, judging
nobody, drenching the thick mulch of dead leaves,
soaking the trees, filling the gullies and crannies of the
wood with water, washing out the places where men
have stripped the hillside. What a thing it is to sit
absolutely alone in the forest at night, cherished by this
wonderful, unintelligent perfectly innocent speech, the
most comforting speech in the world. . . . Nobody
started it, nobody is going to stop it. It will talk as long
as it wants, the rain. As long as it talks I am going to
listen.
                                        Thomas Merton

"Everything dies, baby, that's a fact. But
baby, everything that dies, some day, comes back."
Bruce Springsteen

Alix makes caustic remarks about
Bruce Springsteen while I listen with a
lump in my throat. Different generations, class
stuff and something about queerness, butch
personas and that whole urban thing.
Junior lies beside me on the bed playing with
his fingers and making these small conversational
noises that make me smile. Sometimes
these days I feel as if I have come
to a whole new level in my life, understand
things I never thought about before.
I look at Junior and my stomach goes
tight with fear for him. What if?
What if he gets sick or there's something
wrong with him? I think of Melvin
Dixon and start to cry, seeing his mother's
grief and fear. I look at Alix watching
Junior smile and my lungs fill up so
full my heart hurts. Pride? Joy?
Sheer swelling love, and behind it always
the fear of losing her. Loving someone is
about the fear of losing them, death always
kicking at the door, but also the simple slow
attrition of life itself. Babies grow up,
lovers get moody, work eats you up.
I have to hang onto this sense of joy, this
deep physical happiness, I ignore the fear.

<u>Sunday</u>   <u>May 23, 1993</u>

So yesterday was our *fun* day according to our new schedule. Actually worked out pretty well, though once again I was so exhausted by evening that I had turned into a zombie and had to lie down for an hour to get through till we could put Junior to bed, and fall out beside him. Of course, he woke up at 6:30 this morning ready to start the day and had to be painfully persuaded that, *no*, it was not really day and he *had* to go back to sleep. Moments later the dog started trying to eat the bed. I crawled down painfully an punched her in the face so that she slunk away and I could pass out again. Junior slept on, till 10:30! Neither Alix nor I could believe it.

Both of us woke up feeling hungover, achey and full of congestion, the animals desperate to be fed and Junior hungry as well. Not much recovered now, though I have made breakfast, washed dishes and had a bath, and Alix is even now vacumning the whole house.

Last night, lying restless but exhausted, I found myself thinkging about a novel, *Starrett Hill*, like **Linden Hills**, the novel by Gloria Naylor, but a trash class white people's novel, a different thing altogether. The image in my mind was one from yesterday down in Villa Grande when we were driving around the little windy, pine needle lanes near the post office there. I saw this man from behind, walking away from us like a broken-down John the Baptist with long gray shaggy hair and a dull grey-black coat over worn out jeans, so worn they no longer had any color but dust. He kept his head down so there was no way to see his eyes or his features really, only that shrugged and sunken posture that said everything. If we moved over there we would be looking down on that town--not a town really but a settlement--like an early version of a poverty-stricken Berkeley. In the novel I was as broken down as he, hips and legs crushed in some unnamed accident, vaguely guilty and resentful, full of rage as I always am anyway. Memory and place spilled over me. Cais and Larry raising their boys, Jay telling herself lies, Conley going slow mad next door, Stacey and Jon already fully disconnected from reality. "We're not like anybody else," they keep saying in the book, "it's not the same as with straight people." Jan's brother wearing Bo's caustic sense of humor and resentment. Xmas walking through telling her terrible stories, John Paul and his boyfriend wrestling in the road, the bourgie boys from down the street bicycling by in the height of faggot fashion, aerostreamed thighs pumping. Yes, a novel about the hill. Let it cook for a while.

How are my sisters I wonder? Has Barbara lost her mind again? Has Mandy left? No where to go, of course. She could be me. I could have been her. Thank you god for what was not as I forgive you for what was. ...Do I have the right to forgive god?

Yesterday we went to Santa Rosa and rented Alix a trombone. She had already sent in her registration to Santa Rosa Junior College, will be taking music theory Monday, Wednesday and Fridays from 9 to 10 am.

Nick Dolan (212-5~~60-2989~~) called to ask me to speak about book stuff on Charlie Rose this thursday morning. It would mean getting up at 8:30 and being conscious and articulate. They're going to have the author of the award-winning *Common Ground*, Jay McEnerny John Leonard, Harry Evans of Random House, and Cris Dawl--an agent from ICM as well as a few others. Old JohnGresham and I are to be called and asked what we're reading and looking forward to this fall.

What?

Lots, because I'm a compulsive reader and because all these people keep sending me gallies and copies of books.
A certain amount of mind candy. I read *The Pelican Brief* on a plane in June and liked it so much I picked up all the others in paperback and am saving them for time off. I generally don't read mysteries but I like mass-market adventures and Stephen King for when I'm just too tired for anything else, or for when the baby's restless from teethin, and I sit up and read while holding him. I'm saving *Needful Things* by Stephen King as a reward for when I finish these essays.

I'm reading *Pigs in Heaven* by Barbara Kingsolver becuase I love everything she does, and this is a treat.

I've just finished:

On The Seventh Day, God Created The Chevrolet by Sylvia Wilkinson--first thing I've read by her but I generally read anything Algonquin Books publishes.

Free Enterprise by Michelle Cliff, about Mary Ellen Pleasant the wealthy black woman from San Francisco who helped finance John Brown. I really love the way Michelle Cliff writes, just the most beautiful language telling terrible stories.

Come to Me by Amy Bloom, just marvelous short stories for when I am feeling bad about the world.

A Year of Rhymes, Bernard Cooper's first novel, becuase I loved *Maps to Anywhere*, his book of short stories.

Been rereading *Lover* by Bertha Harris for about the ninth time, after writing about her for the Village Voice.

The Wives of Bath, a novel by Susan Swan from Knopf, beautifully written and a great narrator but maddening for how it uses the central character--a young woman who masquerades as a boy, wants to be a boy, is in love with another girl and winds up killing the one man who has been kind to her and cutting off his penis so she pretend it is hers.

Sunday Night January 2nd.

Read the manuscript of _The Gift of the Body_
by Rebecca Brown. Simply a masterpiece —
very simply. Simple story, language, emotion,
honesty and insight. And beautiful like
life and death and loss — the whole complicated
marvel of the body itself. I think about
Mamma's body, the heat draining out of it
with the end of the struggle. So big,
that pain and the ache that follows,
the ache that proves the body existed
is important, was and was not the life.

Full of slow marvel.

2 men arrested for rape, death of cross-dresser

ASSOCIATED PRESS

HUMBOLDT, Neb. — A woman who posed as a man and dated women was found shot to death with two other people two weeks after residents of this rural area learned her true identity.

Two men accused of sexually assaulting Teena Brandon were arrested for investigation of murder.

Friends said Brandon, 21, had posed for two months as a man named Brandon Teena and had told various stories of having an incomplete sex-change operation.

SAN FRANCISCO EXAMINER
A-8 Sunday, January 2, 1994 ★ ★ ★ ★

A child murdered
for what? Offending
the midwestern moral
mind? And killed it?
Who? the people — who?
male or female? Queer?
the story behind the story
is the one I want to
know.

Saturday   **February 26, 1994**

Ordered a catalog from *The Naughty Victorian*, at 2315-B Forest Drive, Suite 68H, Annapolis, MD 21401. My my.

Audio Books, Blackstone Audio Books, Box 9969, Ashland OR 97520, 1-800-~~729-2565~~.

When I am dead, make of my skin a sounding board. Drum out hope where

there was none before. Make a timpani of my bones and despair. Go past shame and

remember me as I truly was, child of a family not meant to survive who lived anyway.

Remember me, the one who loved well the women in her life.

Tuesday   **March 1, 1994**

Got the TV back from Alpha Electronics (~~542-8563~~) and the boom box back from Good Guys. Otherwise, spend the entire day lying about being weak and sweaty, or sleeping. Don't know if it was eating pizza without eating milk pills or lack of sleep or stress, or everything together, but I was completely useless. Barely managed to care for Junior last night, telling him repeatedly "Mommy has an owie".

This morning I have been doing business. Talked to Laquita Vance and I will meet her Sunday at 10 am (408-~~624-5956~~) at Claudia's.

Called back Robin Desser, *Vintage Books*, 212-5~~32-7438~~ and left a message. She's the editor of the new edition of The Redneck Way of Knowledge. Called Chesley of *Northlight Books*, 5~~29-950~~, H-5~~98-7705~~. Set up a gig there for June 27th, a Monday night, but Alix said maybe we could get a baby-sitter for Wolf and she could drop me off, or I could take him with me. Maybe.

Spoke to Nancy who has been working on some book on girls and horses which she expects to sell well but who she has been having trouble with in the editing. Result is she raved about working with me. She also said Robin is not feeling well and hasn't been for a while, but is only this week going to a doctor. Nancy seems to have an anxious aura about that. Hope it is just too much stress. After all the girlfriend has moved, taken a new job, bought a house and fallen in love--all in a short period of time. High Stress all around.

Other business. Alix spoke to Paul Signorelli at the *SF Public library*, 415-~~891-4780~~. I signed the *Glamour* contract and returned it to Frances. Called Frances and asked about Rochester since I need to do a gig for the Women's Building in May or June.

Now I just need to make local Eye and Dentist appointments and I will feel in control. Also get the cottage organized, the laundry folded and my nerves set for caring for Junior tonight while Alix is in Healdsburg. Tomorrow night is her concert.

The air is so thick I seem to push through syrup. My back hurts and my eyes are thick and heavy. I do these gigs and I use myself up — looking women in the eye trying to get them to talk. Feel like I am always balancing assuming my stance, trying to be ready to move in the direction needed. Trying not to put on too much of a public face. Not make too many jokes.

These children look at me like I am some mama hen come to brood their eggs. I take a deep breath and try.

I give them a terminate exercise knowing that is not enough time. But maybe they will begin.

Writers write. Really do it begin to hear themselves fall in love with their own voices.

Po Bronson

I met Nina ten years ago. On our first date I pulled out all these little slips of pastel-colored paper that I'd stolen from the card catalog in Green Library at Stanford. She was worried I would lose them. The next day she gave me my first notebook. Although there have been close calls, in those ten years I've never lost a notebook.

Bombardiers germinated in my spiral-bound notebooks for six months before I started the first draft, which then took four months to complete. The two phases are very distinct. I jot down ideas and make diagrams until I feel the story is ready to burst—until I'm naively convinced that all the loose ends are tied up and the story has a compelling urgency to be written down. Then I go for it.

I started taking notes in my regular 5½-by-8½ spiral-bound notebooks. The enclosed excerpts are taken from that period. When I knew I was going to write this book, I purchased an oversized 9-by-12 spiral book with unlined paper. I broke all of my plotlines into their triggering points, and wrote down all of these scenes on Post-its. I stuck all the Post-its in the big notebook in chronological order. In the corner of every Post-it, I cross-indexed scenes by characters and subject category (the book's chapters open with nonfiction commentaries). This gave me three ways to jump from scene to scene, rather than just chronologically. My goal was to stomp back and forth over the material, using each scene only once, and to hit every scene before I finished—like Twister, the party game with colored circles on the ground.

Po Bronson is associate publisher of Mercury House in San Francisco. His first novel, Bombardiers, *was published by Random House.*

To help me concentrate—to keep me true to the vision I had when I started the draft—I wrote this novel while locked inside the supply closet of Nina's home office. The closet is twenty-two inches wide. By way of comparison, my shoulders are about twenty-four inches wide, which means I now walk around hunchback. The supply shelf was only two inches above my head, and while sitting upright in a metal folding chair, I could reach past my Mac and touch the far wall. I spent eighteen weeks in there, mornings and nights, with the keyboard on my lap and the monitor providing the only light. I was writing about our obsession with work, and my experiences in the closet provided plenty of material.

I was completely free of distractions, and the only reference materials I kept in there were my notebooks and Tim O'Brien's *Going After Cacciato*. After writing a chapter, I would outline what I had actually written on an index card and tape it to the wall. Then I would open my notebook and cross off the Post-it scenes I had managed to include.

This past fall I discovered 2½-by-5-inch, ruled "Stealth" notebooks. They fit into any pocket and are less conspicuous to write in. However, their small size makes them much easier to misplace. Nina thinks they are too unsafe for the storage of precious thoughts, but several times we have been at a lecture or a reading and something triggers a thought in her head. I can see the panic in her eyes as she realizes that she has been caught without paper. I lord it over her, make her beg me for a spare page.

I was always told to "write about what you know." All it seemed I knew about was what it was like to try to find time around my job to write, so that led to a few metafictional stories about being a writer. Finally, it occurred to me to write about work itself—to explore why my wife and I seem to work so hard and the effect work has on us. I'd studied economics in college. In the process of making the diagram on the next pages, I achieved, quite literally, a personal enlightenment. Later, I came back to this diagram to make an essay of it that would serve as the book proposal.

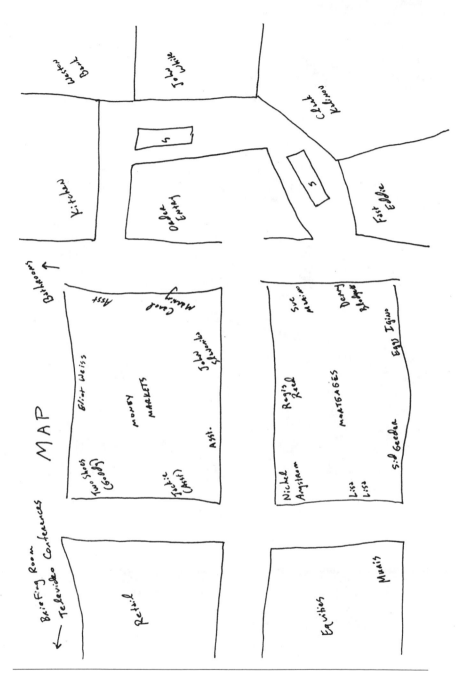

I drew this diagram of my imagined sales floor. It helped me visualize. I was afraid an office was too familiar to the reader, so I consciously decided to explode the level of detail, to render each of their desks so acutely that this particular workplace would verge on the grotesque—to the point of making the reader uncomfortable.

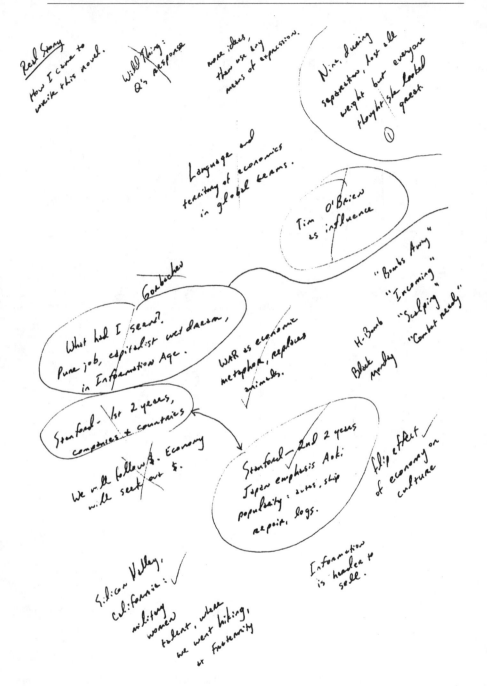

Real Story
How I came to write this novel.

Will Bing: Q's response

more ideas, then use any means of expression.

Nine, during separation, lost all weight but everyone thought she looked great

Language and territory of economics in global terms.

Tim O'Brien as influence

"Bombs Away"
"Incoming"
H-Bomb "Scalping"
Black Monday "Combat ready"

Gorbachev
What had I seen? Pure job, capitalist wet dream, in Information Age.

WAR as economic metaphor, replaces animals.

Stanford - 1st 2 years, companies + countries

We will follow $. Economy will seek out $.

Stanford - 2nd 2 years Japan emphasis Aoki: popularity: autos, ship repair, logs.

flip effect of economy on culture

Silicon Valley: California: military women talent, where we went hiking, ex-Fraternity

Information is harder to sell.

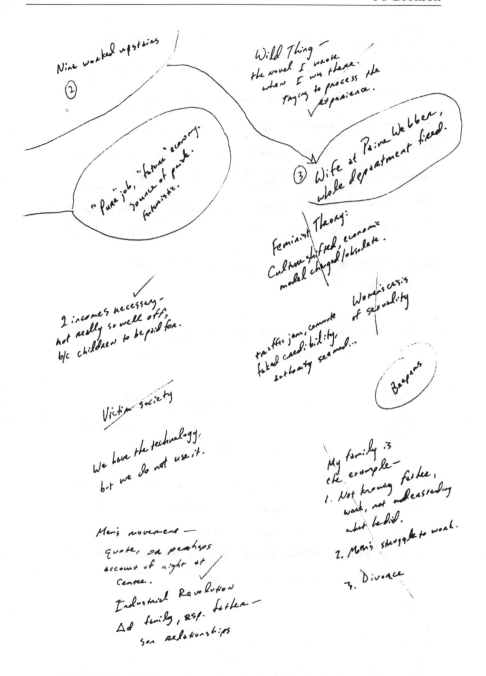

I made a list of what my fraternity brothers were doing with their lives. The last paragraph reads, "Everyone wasted their talent. While we becry the failure to educate our workforce, the most educated of our workforce become part of the sideshow."

- In training program, like Yossarian & Clevinger in basic training. Classes. Interviewed by departments for jobs, all thinking they're the best. Never answering a question in interviews. Proving eccentricity. Wanting to sell. They want me to say "feel it in your gut," or "instinct." Similarity to the way cults recruit, promising wealth & friendship & no commitment, then requiring a lot later.

- Each of their stories, but still Yossarian is protagonist.

- Other absurdities thrown in: other government involvement:
   — paying people to not grow alfalfa.

Finance absurdities
Gameboy, supernintendo int'l trade.

- We "glorified" captains of industry as we used to glorify soldiers. Bold, striking moves, not the bureaucracy it really is. War writing transformed our perception of war & battle. Many showed it was horrible — Catch 22 showed its absurdity, its bureaucracy, its bloated silliness.

Nina and I went to Zihuatanejo for five days to take a break. For no real reason I packed along *Catch-22*, one of the only books I'd read in college. Heller blasts apart the glorification of war and its generals. I'd been thinking of writing something based on my two years working at First Boston selling bonds. In *Catch-22*, I saw a way to debunk the view of business as the domain of well-mannered captains of industry. I saw a way to write about business from the trenches rather than the boardroom.

4 Days a week plan:

Option 1: help me when I'm there.

Computer workstation: put most DTP on Mac. Accounting on PC. Share office space?

What I do:

Bills stuff
   help w/ software

Trouble
foreign payments, lawsuits

Accounting
  Royalties (Ag w/ diversity)
  Pay bills
  Deposit checks
  Post journals

Year End
  inventory
  writedowns
  COGS
  AP

Planning
  budgeting

CBSD
  Loans
  New pubs
  Legal matters

Bank contract
Decisions on all matters
computer distribution?

DTP / PRODUCTION, MKTG

new software, fonts
typeset 4 books/season
typeset catalog
typeset intros, etc.

design, produce all ads
produce direct mailers
program databases

As the reality of writing a novel began to take hold, I started to panic about how to find the time to write it. This is a list of my job responsibilities. I was trying to work up the courage to ask my employer for a four-day workweek.

Needs a person

Lost identity in job

Implicit first person narrator,
be a little more implicit. Use
this to draw in after beguab
wears off.

Regret. On otherside. Was in it,
now out.

Who is talking is the suspense
action.

2 days to tell whole story of
why they ended up in loony
bin. Can't wait to end. Every
small piece replicates the
whole.

TIMELESS, NON-RETRO

Separate elements

Remove details of the 80s.

We respond to the human
elements of their story,
not the exposé of Finance.

We live in an inhuman world.

Machine of business.

Work makes people sick.

This is what it's about.

Could be any industry.

Strength - rapid fire
inclusive style. Distinctive
qualities are strengths

AVOID PERIOD

- don't worry about being elegiac,
nodding back to the 80s. We know
what we expect to think — plunge
into reality of job life, diff't
speed than human life.

IDENTIFY NARRATOR

tell everything in every moment
"We were all going to hell."

SHOULDN'T BE VERY LONG

180 pgs.
not enough stamina for reader.

PLOT

A last man standing story
who will last longer?

Need character who totally
loves it.

Form and content meet in pace.

Life's pace.

Text's pace.

Huge breaths between
paragraphs.

I was still on the fence whether to take on the workload. Four months
previously, I had written a short story using some of the characters I wanted to
include in the novel, and I had sent this short story to Walter Kirn in Montana.
Walter finally called me back and was excited about the story. I told him I'd
been thinking of making it a novel, and I think he, more than anyone, saw how
it might work. Spontaneously, I wrote on these Post-its as he talked about the
possibilities. His encouragement put me over the hump.

- The activity could come from anywhere. These were all things to contend with:

There were bursts of activity, and then the smoke cleared and we hunkered back in. Sometimes the activity picked up again, and we shouted and screamed and ran about frantically. Sometimes we settled for days, waiting always for the next hit. When the lights lit up, we yelled "Incoming" and grabbed our headsets and phones. We punched up the Treasury market on one screen, ~~Equity~~ Mortgage brokers on another, and money market offerings on a third. We yelled out market positions like coordinates. We got on our walkie-talkies. This was pre-dawn. We were up in the middle of the night, throwing out our sales pitches, dumping our ~~bonds~~ bombs.

The activity could come from anywhere, anytime. First, there was politics to watch.

Read 1984 again.

I was waiting for the first lines to come into my head, or at least their tone and feel. I can't explain it, but many ideas always come to me while I'm driving my scooter to work. It probably creates the right amount of nonverbal background stimulation, or something. One mile of driving and I'm caught between the need to stop (to write down my thought) and the desire to keep driving (to see what else comes). On this day, I pulled over on Masonic, above the municipal bus lot. It never reads on paper as well as it sounded in my head.

ETHAN CANIN

I get my best ideas while driving, especially driving at night, and often write them down on a notepad that sticks to the windshield with a suction cup. From there they go into my wallet, where they sit for months until the next time I look. By then they have faded and taken on the curve of my thigh, but I can also see whether they are any good or just the product of nighttime enthusiasm. One of the more difficult parts of writing is making the transition from an idea, which usually arrives with exhilaration, to a story, which must pass before the merciless eyes of the internal literary inspector—it's maudlin; there's no plot; it's nothing but a gimmick.

Once I start writing, however, I don't look at my notes. They're mostly an impetus to begin; if I work too close to them, I lose the ability to imagine. Every day I write one idea—usually a scene or an event—and then I quit. Sometimes when I'm feeling very productive, I'll make a list of assignments for myself at the end of a session—scenes to write later when I can't think of anything on my own.

Occasionally I write notes in the hospital, but this is fairly rare. Usually there's not enough time, not to mention the fact that you're thinking in an utterly different way—you don't see a man lying in the bed, you don't see a human being contemplating his own imminent and painful death, you see a body with a T-helper-cell count of zero and a headache that could be meningitis. And you're thinking, it's past midnight and I'd better do a lumbar puncture before morning.

Ethan Canin lives in San Francisco. He is the author of Emperor of Air *and* Blue River *(both Houghton Mifflin). His most recent collection is* The Palace Thief *(Random House).*

Po— Softball at 5:00. Great Meadow,
Ft. Mason.

I'm on jury duty

which the trivial is defended by the socialist-realist rationalization that it's supposed to be that way because that's the way we really are!

The New Yorker has thus become the reincarnation of the nineteenth-century French Academy, promoting one school of fiction to the exclusion of all others. As a prominent *New Yorker* editor once told me, "God, we publish pages and pages of drivel every week." He then went on to brag that he'd rejected some excellent writers, apparently pleased, for example, that he'd had a chance to turn down Ethan Canin's stuff.

TALENT POOLS TALENT PC

M.F.A. programs have become the stocked ponds of our most prestigious publishing houses—places where writers... 3. Susan Mi... *Stories*, Hou... 4. Jill Eisens... dom House...

674
01742

NOVEL IDEA

SMALL POX
narrator: County Doc

Narrator is
optimist?
[illegible]

Black kid in
white kindergarten
class— Nasty kid—
obscene gestures—
Suburban narrator—
argues c̄ wife— goes
to see kid, takes him
out; kid disappears; maybe
shows up one day at
night.

```
other ideas:
Which Among You Shall Betray Me
The Life of a Despot
A Man I Saw in Darkness
A Knife in March
A Student of Dream and Treachery
In View of the Palace
A Student of History
The Palace Thief
The Palace Viper
```

ASSIGNMENTS:

1. RICH WOMAN FLIRTS WITH HIM

2. GOES HOME WITH ANOTHER WOMAN, WHERE HE FINDS THE HUSBAND
HAVING AN AFFAIR. BRINGS THE MEAT HOME AND STICKS IN IN HIS
FREEZER.

3. SEES A GIRL HE WENT TO HIGH SCHOOL WITH. HEY, NAN, HE SAYS,
IT'S MARTY Deel. I DON'T REMEMBER YOU, SHE SAYS. THE NEXT DAY
SHE TELLS HIM SHE DID REMEMBER HIM. OR ELSE: SEES A GIRL HE WENT
OT HIGH SCHOOL WITH, BUT IS EMBARRASSED TO ACKNOWLEDGE HER. GIVE
HER A TENTH OF A POUND EXTRA AND WONDERS IF SHE KNEW IT WAS HE.

4. GOES OUT WITH LINA. LINA WORKS AT BOEING IN PERSONNEL, BUT
TODAY SHE IS LAID OFF.

5. MARTY BRINGS OVER THE STEAKS HE'S GOT FROM THE WOMAN.

6. MOTHER CALLS HIM AT HOME. HOW'S THE TECHNOLOGY? GREAT, IT'S
A PEN-BASED COMPUTING COMPANY. HOW COME MRS. MILLER SAID YOU
SOLD HER GROUND ROUND.

7. RECOGNIZES PEOPLE ALL OVER TOWN. WOMAN HUGS HIM AT THE
COUNTER AND HE DOESN'T KNOW WHO SHE IS. TURNS OUT TO BE MRS.
MILLER.

8. GOES HOME, WETS HIS HANDS AT THE HOSE AND KISSES HER. "i MUST
HAVE FORGOTTEN TO WASH MY HANDS," HE SAYS

Considers stealing the car, when he finds the keys in his pocket later.

Tone down the McNaught meeting. Actually, make her say a lot of disconcerting things, like about blood on the seat.

Flash in family remembrances to make the end more poignant, about his parent's wasted lives.

Play up the stealing of meat.

A Spy in His Own Land
You Can't Teach a Genius Anything
Genius

time in which my own heart would break like a china bowl, and
would stay broken for a long time before it it ever realigned.

The Pieces of My Heart

of my own years of envy and spite.

My brother was known secretly in our famiily as a genius; high
scores, low grades; real fuck-up; I did well; He does drug-
related things and begins to write his own dictionary; brother
begins to hear about it--it begins to gain credence in the
neighborhood, people begin to talk in their language; one day
brother goes in to destroy it but can't, being so moved by the
hundreds of its pages; instead he steals it;

he keeps his girlfreind in a secret fort in the basement; mother
notices missing blankets (they are g.f.'s bed); brother plays
rock music, younger brother tries playing piano with it;

father tries to get them to play ping-pong as a family sport;
younger brother plays and gets good, older brother refuses;
father forces him to play; serves balls that hit him; finally
gives up; then y.b. plays ping pong with dad whenever o.b. is in
fort with girlfriend; one day exposed the fort by hitting a long
pingpong slam;

father has them read the newspaper every morning as togetherness;
we could pick our own papers; first he read Rolling Stone and
then High Times; I read the Christian Science Monitor because our
librarian, Mrs. Geldin, recommended it

when they finally play ping-pong, have brother hold the paddle
chinese style.

Clive invents a language;

he finds Clive sitting naked with Bart, his friend in the fort,
with Maria behind them;

only a vindictive pleasure at which I am now ashamed, and a view

or at least that there was something both forgiving and conspiratorial # at the heart of our relationship—and that for this I can no longer see him in any light but the one in which I now recall him: an eccentric

How do you make your peace with the memory ... did things, on might think, unreasonable—hard at the time of ... again ... of a man like that? He did things I did ...

NAME _____
DOA __/__ DOD __/__ CODE _____ 10/18/1926 M 01006450 E 1
CONTACT Son in law 242
MD DAUGHTER 560   Gloria (daughter)
10064500 1320   12/03/9;

ID & CC 67 yo Chinese ♂ c̄ h/o PVD, PROBLEMS *original man, alone*
Dukes B3 Adeno Ca of colon admitted c̄ 1 GI Bleed - *on an abandoned*
melena x 2 day, BRBPR x 1 2 R/O MI - *L. IIItp, went*
3 s/p Liver Ca — *to commit a*
HPI ... epigast. pain x wks/month, relieved 4 Anemia — *crime with*
by Maalox + eating, ∅ hematemesis or emesis; 5 _____ *his son.*
OTC P occ soon c̄ burning abd pain. At Adult Care 6 _____
this AM →NG →BRB →1500 cc NS did not clear; 7 _____
td'd 6L in E.D. 8 _____
Hct 9/93 48. This AM 28. (...) 9 _____
PRE-OP CEA's <1.0 10 _____
(+) squeezing chest pain s̄ radiation, lasts, 1 mm; ∅ palp 11 _____
∅ SOB; Pain on exertion + sitting down; 12 _____
S.P.-Duke's B c̄ Positive Margins 13 _____
HCT 28-72 →IVF →720 1900→3 FeH for UGIB 14 _____
PMH 20 to NSAID's for duodenal ulcer
Urology →?reflux c̄ wedge removed from liver; ∅ nodes; poorly diff adeno
PSH Colectomy 1988 Radiation; Cholecystectomy; ∅ recurrence;
FHx
TOB ∅   EtOH ∅   DRUGS ∅   (LU) _____
SOCIAL ...
ALLERGY ∅
MEDS Carafate
Maalox
_____

ROS _____
90 102   PE: VS T ___ BP 126/62 HR 94 RR 16 O2Sat 100 4L
56 c̄   GEN
SKIN (+)spider, (+)duputrens, palmar erythema
HEENT
9/93 HCT 48   NECK supple   BACK
HCT: #1:27.5 9:30   CHEST ... Rt ?↓BS ↓ base
#2:20.4 ... IVF   COR S S₂ ... m
#3: 19   ABD vertical scar, ∅ H-sm   RECTAL heme(+)
#4   GU
EXT
NEURO
LABS: CXR _____   EKG ∅ ST/T Δ's, rate 100

PT 11.7/25.0   142|106|37 < 215   115 > 73 / 19 \ 166
                 4.4|29|1.1

Diff. _____   Ca 8.3   AlkP ____
26 / 11   PT/PTT 11.7/1.0/25   Mg ____   PO₄ ____
2.0 X   ABG _____   Amy 59   Osm ____
0.3   U/A _____   ESR ____   TP ____
           LP _____   Alb 2.5   Glb ____
           KUB _____   UrA ____
           BCx _____   UCx ____   SpCx ____
           CK/LD _____   Other CEA (+); Fibrinogen 250
PREVIOUS LABS
__/__ _____   __/__ _____

Bld o (+)

Meds: Omeprazole 20gD Acyclover 800 5,5d
Keflex (Cellulitis) 500mg x10 days
trazodone 50 qhs   Natural tears T̄ 5,5d
Septra
Itraconazole
Prozac
SHx: lives alone in Diamond Hts;
All: PCN → rash

PE
Abd ∅ heme ⊕ c̄ streaky stool

9/15 CryAS⊖

LDH 522

Meds   1) orthostasis
C̄ hidu
Omeprazole   2) Bell's; BLP
Acyclovir 800 5xD   - eye → patch
Itra   ophtha
Septra   3) Cellulitis
Prozac
                        4) KS

HU c̄ I.D.
1 wk +
Parallel story   Oncology mt
of four active   Th... +
separate incidents GI
being picked up by 5) GI —
strangers — th   omeprazole
tension implicit in GI hx poss.
that. Some work   of scope
out, one is horrific 6) HIV
All kinds of b... M. in Septra tension
and attention to small acts
                    + detail.

KAREN CLARK

I have kept notebooks for many years, mostly college-ruled spiral notebooks that are fairly unstructured. When a notebook is going particularly well, it ends by simply reaching the last piece of paper, at which point the cover may be attached with tape, paper clips, even staples. Other notebooks are less successful, rarely flow from page to page, and remain unfinished. These notebooks are heartbreaking to find in drawers.

Most often the notebooks carry a mixture of journal entries and drafts of poems. In this notebook I found myself following several unwritten rules: only write in pencil; never tear any paper out for other uses; and respect the number of pages in each section, as well as where each section ends, even though it may create a strange effect on the piece being written. This is a three-subject notebook, and each appearance of the cardboard divider forced a breakthrough of ideas about where and how to begin with the poems on the other side of the cardboard. I have learned to respect the element of chance in sudden endings.

Most of the following pages revolve around my current manuscript, one driven partially by various resonances of a wolf archetype. In working in this particular notebook I often came up against trying to map out a lineage, a string, a musical sequence. Simultaneously I found myself writing a series of entries, more like prose poems, that were either written or typed and then stapled into the notebook. A final version was then typed on onionskin and put in a folder. This has become almost a complementary series to the other poems being written. Since the notebook still seems to be an intrinsic part of the poems and I am sure that there will be more maps, more sequences, I am not sure whether this notebook has ended. There are eight sheets of paper left.

Karen Clark directs the California Readings/Workshops Program for Poets & Writers and lives in San Francisco.

7/24 I need the desire for exploration, for belief even in the presence of august disbelief. I need to remember the eyes of a dog versus the eyes of a wolf. I feel the finger of a wolf and the hands of a dog, I love the dog and hate the wolf. I am the wolf. He is the wolf. What is the desire between wolf and dog, to end as the wolf dog? Untrainable, strange, difficult results. To think of how I dreamed of this so many autumns ago, his hand over me, tender and strange. The music was effortless. The prince + the princess were sad + insane. They had some wolves in the castle. The dogs and the wolves wandered so. The bodies filled the tapestry and so it was that the story began.

7/31

Here is a revision of the manuscript order/ideas, extra notes.

1) need to work on the first wolves, memories leading into animals cration of wolf; influences; history—add factual information?

2)need to work on literal journey, north to south, but maybe also midwest to north

3) Psych institute—work with the idea of ten; need to make it surreal enough so as to lessen impact of stereotype, need to maybe explore of admitted wolf, mother, female wolves, caretakers, sick wolves

4) poem about the Sleep is connected to Final Solution; similar imagery, sub/unconcious? how to connect ?

5) like original idea about encounter with memory?watching wolves, bobcats, coyotes—maybe compare /contrast this with psych institute, memory regained that way, or not as in some cases; obliteraiton of memory

6) need to play up factual history; wolves being destroyed by ranchers; hybrids not accepted—dogs and woyotes whoa re they? what do they represent?

8) need to move psychologicval landscape forward, out of literal and into abstract; how does

9) Idea of the forces; avoid Plath / Roethke / Lowell

and the tension, and my writing, and
my new imaginary friend. Who is in
fact imaginary.

The cycles are winding down. There
is extreme paranoia on my part, an
overactive imagination. It needs to be
quelled. [Quell: to thoroughly overwhelm and
reduce to submission or passivity.]

For the air has opened and this
figure, this tiresome and driest, most
forbidding technical music — It needs
to be written. And here are some new
notes for it: Or questions:

1) what is the main line, melody, etc.
going to be? What will c) form
and b) subject be?

2) what will 2nd + 3rd voices be?

3) How to interpret music, voices, harmonies
of wolves, etc. (plus form, inherent) of figure
AND 2nd more impt meaning — disturbed
state of consciousness — acts in which
I appear to be conscious but then
cannot remember when I come to;

Dear wolf: It seems I have abandoned you. In fact I
return out of confusion and agony. I know only you,
the way you stared and then turned on me. I remember
it so clearly, with much difficulty. But then I found
I have written these lines: So returns the image of the
wolf. Because I am only free with the wolf. I'm not
sure what else I can say but that.

It is true. I have come into a clearing with another,
and stood my ground. He blinked, and may disappear.
Where shall I ever find him again? Does he want me
to find him again. I don't know. Do I turn back or
keep going? Do I fight if he fights, or do I just
wait patiently until he is again calm. The clearing
suddenly seems so wide, expansive. With you wolf
the violence and stillness was everywhere. Here there
is mostly kindness and gentleness, except for this last
bout which was rather frightening. I don't expect
you to tell me anything wolf; for you merely like to
humiliate me over and over, and I'm not staying long
enough for that.

1/18

KATHERINE DUNN

Some of these notes are on envelopes or other scrap paper, but most are pages from all-purpose 6-by-9 notebooks that I carry until they're full and then pitch into a box. Everything goes into these notebooks. Phone numbers and lists of chores (garbage out, bathe dog, etc.), journalistic interviews, notes on boxing matches, graffiti seen, conversations overheard, mindless doodling while on hold. Also included are ideas about the novel I'm working on.

This isn't a sophisticated process. These notes exist because thinking about a project doesn't all take place during specified, official writing time. You grab ideas when they come, and they come oddly, triggered by anything, because the novel is always in the back of your head. You stop in the middle of washing dishes, dry your hands enough to prevent smeared ink, and make a note in barely functional code to remind you later. Your dinner partner heads for the rest room, and you whip out the notebook to jot some revelation while he's gone. An image on the TV news kicks in and you miss the rest because you're scribbling. A scene through a bus window leads to jagged scratches—illegible because the bus is moving.

Some notes are the product of deliberate research—call an expert or run into one in a bar, ask about sniper scopes, techniques of taxidermy, etc. (Notes on written material—books and periodicals—are taken in meticulous crabbed form on legal pads.)

Every week or so I comb through the current notebook and copy over anything that still seems to have possible value, typing slightly more complete versions into my computer in endless, disorganized files named "Notes." Some get moved later to the pertinent sections of the novel I'm working on. They don't get organized in any form until then, but I know where they go. Others get abandoned as stupid or irrelevant.

Katherine Dunn lives in Portland, OR. Knopf published her third novel, Geek Love, *nominated for the National Book Award for Fiction. The pages that follow are selected from notebooks kept over the last half of 1992 for a novel-in-progress,* Cut Man.

mead   59604   Management Series™

RFB's Diary

+ Degas + modigliani

I kill men for the same reason Botticelli painted
women — because they are beautiful to me. And mysterious.
Their clean lines are grace and strength to me.

I make a sharp distinction between boys
and Men — The one lean to the point of neutrality,
hairless. The child version almost genderless and
usually unthreatening.

The real challenge and fascination is with the
full blown adult male — heavy chested, thick
necked, full bearded and hairy bodied
Zeus or Poseidon — powerful, dangerous and
protective.

She Bites/Personalities
  A) she isn't like this at home - stays the same
  B) clothes available influenced the roll
  C) if she had to carry one persona too long she'd
     slip - grow impatient at having to hide so
     much for so long/
                    her dark side during the clown phase
  D) The rolls alternated — often the drab drone
     would be the transition between two vivid I.D.'s
     more than once xcept for the "Nice, Pretty Girl"

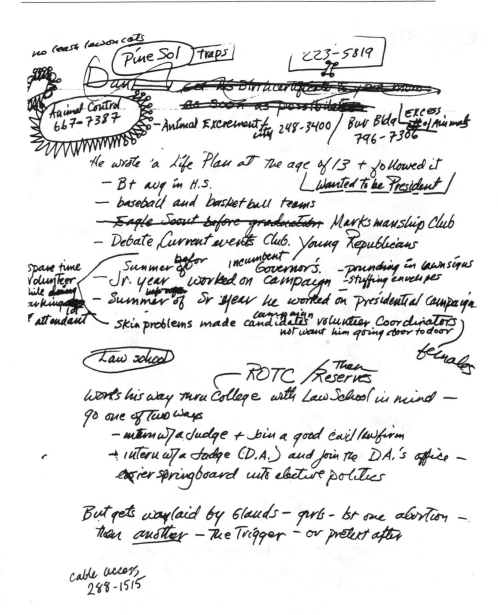

no least lawon cats

Pine Sol traps   223-5819

Dan

Animal Control
667-7387   —Animal Excrement city 248-3400 / Bur Bldg EXCESS
                                            796-7306 #of Animal

He wrote a Life Plan at the age of 13 + followed it
   — B+ avg in H.S.   Wanted to be President
   — baseball and basketball teams
   — Eagle Scout before graduation Marksmanship Club
   — Debate, Current events Club. Young Republicans

spare time   Summer befor incumbent Governor's. —pounding in lawn signs
volunteer   —Jr. year worked on campaign —stuffing envelopes
while doing — Summer of Sr year he worked on Presidential campaign
working a   skin problems made candidates volunteer Coordinators)
attendant   campaign not want him going door to door

Law school   females
                —ROTC / Reserves Then
works his way thru College with Law School in mind —
go one of two ways
   — intern w/a Judge + join a good civil lawfirm
   + intern w/a Judge (D.A.) and join the DA.'s office —
   easier springboard into elective politics

But gets waylaid by Glands — girls — 1st one abortion —
then another — The Trigger — or pretext after

cable access,
288-1515

RB re Leo / as soon as she saw him
she knew it would be a sad story

● Lucy — would have an inward, listening
air — distracted — unattached to the hurly-
burly around her
— she resisted exercise of any kind on the
grounds that the violence of muscle use
could screen important data — that the
small pings and twangs of muscle strains
resulting from such weighty action as sweeping,
climbing stairs or folding laundry could
confuse the messages vibrating through her
flesh — her body was not a temple but
a measuring device, a delicately calibrated
instrument. "Asking me to wash dishes is like
using an Oscilloscope or a radio satellite
as a ~~Bulldozer~~ (pounding nails with an
Oscilloscope or plowing
with a radio satellite

digging
ditches)

walking
down the
street to
the grocery
for coffee
+ dish
soap,

She
watches
kids eat
couldn't be expected
to change a diaper,
zip a jacket or
reach all the way across
the table to pour a glass of
milk — she was happy
watching and would talk,
amiably, of things that
fascinated her — "my ones"
Volcanoes, earthquakes, the
Titanic shifting of the earth's
crust on its dark, liquid core
The kids adored her. She never interfered
When they grew too boisterous they
never scolded — only her eyes turned
inward, kids dropping in wondering if
she was engaged in the silence might
be connected to the fine
dry ticking of the skin
about her butt
crack.

— Somebody else is teaching the hockey team to punch

— Leo gets called in to do a seminar on cut care for the S+M leather Dykes

— amat. kids moms don't want 'em around hookers
— wives + girls of boxers + trainers " " " ".."

i.e. Brenda Tarunqe for Jupe- wait for relatives to show
— call Coyote organizer — move up meeting
—

— all men equal/size, age irrelevant
  all fighters
—

— Kind to each other

— no hits without gloves, rules + witnesses
  ∟ only in ring

— Taught one-on-one (not 20 man
  (not 30 in class,   Team-yelled
  yelled at)   at)

— each an individual, following his
  own dream but supporting and
  respectful of every others dream

never mentioned
those who know are too proud,
and would be embarrassed to have
their marshmallow hearts revealed
(Tough guys, after all)
or, often as not, have seen it all
their lives and never notice it —
take it as naturally as air and
wouldn't think to describe it to
a stranger

fighters create a ring + a gym w/ their sweat and
dreams + the smell + sound of it is like nothing else

Remington
700 series
work out

AI MAR
Suggests

use
.308 winchester
cartridge

4 X 12 scope made by
(microdot
norm. telescopic
sight but with
minimum
light would
work excellently

She deliberately doodles in arrows cuz she's read
That people of purpose + ambition do that

his office in basement/house in Vanc. WA - work in Vanc.
shop + party in Ore. across river (WA -no income Tax,
Ore. - no sales tax) she works NIGHTS in a bank in Vane.

(Perlstein re: Gun) he packs letters in plastic ziploc/ Gun, Ammo
getting ready to set out again

                                        always
Trish has a doll collection — dreams of children — That's
what attracted him, finally.

Beaverton Blondes on the bus — Teens. ~~picked up this old man and~~

    I was working the Benson and I went up to his room. We were about halfway there when he had some kind of attack, some kind of fit. I jumped into my clothes (?) and grabbed his wallet + got out of there. I called the hotel desk from the pay phone at the Dakota + told 'em there was a to check him. Then I sat there w/ a coffee + watched the ambulance come in. I put his wallet in a mail box — didn't take his credit cards or I.D. — There was only about $300 in there anyway.

    So this old guy lives. I mean, I saved his life, right? But he presses charges for theft — and sgt. Beader — you know that sonofabitch — he recognizes the old bastard's description + shows up at my door. I tell him exactly what came down. But He hauls me in / I'd just done a speedball — some coke to perk me up and we get there +

One attraction of the True Body as
material is its specificity. The
evident individual identity of The True
Body, is enormously more compelling
and demanding than is The
fabricated image. The very nature.
of the fabricated image is to generalize —
to be open to interpretation, and To apply
to more than one corporeal reality.

A True Body is so explicit that The
whole concept of art as fabrication is
defied and destroyed. This though so
many rules, precepts, of art are obeyed,

You cry when your afraid if you
Cant DO something — that energy
will come out 1 way or another

July 14 - Tuesday
10:36 am   will call from Denver
                to confirm
Continental # 803

Bomb Damage assessment
B.D.A.

Preacher Man Moultrie was doing
push ups in the ring with a shy
3 year old on his back.
~~The~~ preacher had the longest, thinnest
head in Christendom ~~and was~~ wore
~~into to near~~ a wide black ~~hat with~~
~~the ring, within it~~ and a Black robe
into the ring. ~~He~~ would carry a
big ~~family~~ Bible with ribbons
& notes and book marks ~~from~~
between its pages, and he would kneel
in mid-ring and call down
blessings and ~~supply~~ the eye of
god ~~before his bouts.~~ His
manager, M.M.M., encouraged his
behavior as ~~conducive to useful~~
~~& appealing to the crowd and~~
~~either~~ intimidating to his religious superstitious
opponents and ~~deceptive to the~~
Cynics who mistook the Preacher's
~~g~~ reverence for pacifism.
& Promoters liked it — the crazy color
appealed to the crowd but referees above
and commission officials balky

RB's NEA app
   most on Comm think its dull + derivative
   some think it's good
   one thinks it's real
           reject it but send it to Wash. D.C. cops
   in NEA envelope to satisfy the suspicious one
   cops think its art - wasted Tax $
   Toss it - don't even check w/ Oregon or
   anybody

JUAN PABLO GUTIÉRREZ

I have kept diaries for the past thirty years. The following pages contain samples of a unique process that Francisco X. Alarcón, Rodrigo Reyes, and I discovered, a mind-boggling source we call "magic." The three of us came together almost thirteen years ago in the Mission District in San Francisco. We were, to quote a contemporary Chicano poet, "exiles of desire." As Chicano gay males, we were initiated in the world of margins, letters, and cultural politics.

First, we formed a discussion group that dissolved after only a few meetings. Then we proceeded to confront, tear, and disarm each other to the point that we formed a whole of three, a sacred triangle. In doing this, we followed the example of "Las Tres Marías," the three women from Portugal who wrote a book in a single voice more than twenty-five years ago.

Yes, we wanted to shatter the myth of the writer as an individual working in solitude. We saw each other almost every day. We ate, walked, partied, dreamed, and wrote together. We came to recognize the poet, the writer, the artist in each of us as an extension of the other two. In "Triángulo" (an unpublished book) I chronicle this process; it later served as the basis for *Ya vas, carnal* (1985), the first collection of poems written by Francisco, Rodrigo, and me.

My diaries keep a record of life as a miracle—as when a simple regression exercise under the guidance of Lucha Corpi

---

Juan Pablo Gutiérrez is the director of Intercultural Development Associates in San Francisco. He has served as director of the Mission Cultural Center. He co-authored Ya vas, carnal *(Humanizarte, San Francisco). He is the vice-chair of the Bay Area Center for Latino Writers. Rodrigo Reyes, playwright, actor, and director, originally from Texas, founded GALA, the first gay Latino organization in the U.S. Francisco X. Alarcón teaches at the University of California, Davis.*

left Francisco (our greatest skeptic) floored on my living room with a vision of his Mesoamerican past through his third eye. This was the initial impulse that led him to his *Snake Poems* (1992) in which Nahuatl, Spanish, and English become one voice.

For me, the diary is a tool for accessing power. I have come to recognize my diaries as travelogues and oracles that fellow voyagers can consult. Rodrigo Reyes died of AIDS two years ago, but he comes alive again in the pages where he discovers this phrase by St. Francis of Assisi: "What you're looking for is what is looking." As a Chicano Borges, I now question if it was I who wrote the poems Francisco is known for, the same way he could have written this introduction.

06-10→11.89?

Pacho, Miguel (Amellito) y Yo

Pacho trips out on the nail

her B-day → the day Coyolxauhqui stone
was discovered in Templo Mayor & again
trips out when she saw one of the
Copies of 500 years ago was
written by someone named Alarcon.

She read this ——— in the book of
showed him when he came w/ his
gringo students of a trick again
& interrupted us then & he didn't hear
a thing.

corazon

I want the title to be simple, easy to remember, & above all original, I don't want it to be cliché, it can be catchy & simple.

what I want the book to be/do →

1. move away from the old tired rhetoric of my poems

2. to be positive

3. speak of it all through the re-discovery, re-validification of development, actualisation.

4. I want to move clearly into a positive light I want to positive light eminate it shed, radiate

5. I want to speak honestly con mi corazon of in so doing allow it to speak too not as an object but as a living entity one capable of its own everything

not only as a part of a machine!

6. I want to set an example to those who have not done this — really want to know their hearts — not I want to get didactic (rather) I want to do it.

There are to be done though a series of conversations does do

‡ If yo y el hablan → then go on to that one voice.

7. I want to admit my talk about their ✗ ✗ things of the heart merely talked about.

8. I want to be careful not to end unrealistic, empty, redundant o?

cliché words & symbols.

9. I want to get to some other dimension of expression of expression of hopefully do so though the self of (encountering) w/ the new language. An encounter.

10. The positivism, realism, freshness of expression should pre-dominate. The discourse.

11. Explore how uncensoredly the heart & the self are subliminally separated and are made vulnerable to.

todo from society to the
conditioned self image.

12. I want to write this book
for the masses not for
the intellectual few who
will read its forced limited
edition

13. I want every entry (poem) to
capsulate almost graphic art
particle every I want variety of
at least the vast majority of
them should be read quickly
highly impressionate of remembered.

Pancho called this Thurs. re: the 6 page
letter I sent him re: Pantera breaking
in. Pancho still believes, "you, you all
are trying to impose too much order.
What it is, is probably, well, you just don't
understand, you can't accept me anymore having
a little fun ..... (pause) there's nothing wrong
with that!!!" then he added - "to tell you
the truth, I bet the incident w/ Pantera
didn't happen at all - she made it up,
and you, you just added fuel to
the fire Juan Pablo ..... I know that's
exactly what happened."

    then he added - "Well, this is
my call .... I knew what was in the
letter but I still opened it. ... (pause) just
out of curiosity, and I was right - you're
so predictible Juan Pablo - so this is
the script, now I'm supposed to feel
guilty, take the blame - isn't that it,
isn't that the role you I'm supposed to
play?"

    Pancho continues to guilt-trip me
by/w/ repeating (varying)(slightly) the same
statement. When I don't respond, he
abruptly changes the conversation.
    All along as he is talking, in
some parts he speaks louder as or in
order to be heard by someone (probably Sue) who
is in the room w/ him.
    I talk at length w/ Gloria about this.

11.02.83

Read my Diary, what
it will give me are
the KEY message to
incorporate in beginning
prepare to enter a
catalogue Topics in
my Texts & particularly
letter to Fxn or
Chicano Queo Spirituality.
And it append to

Page mirrod draw to
picture Titled "De
Cherrie Moraga, re-interpretiz
for Anglo Audiences
La Loteria."

"La Cherrie Moraga, re-interpreting for Anglo Audiences La Loteria"   Juan Pablo '95   06.14-12.89. F.

EL NOPAL
(THE CACTUS)

BRENDA HILLMAN

*T*he only way to get mystery into a work of art is to let the unconscious do the work it needs to do. That, unfortunately, often takes a little more time—and generally causes more trouble—than working from the conscious mind.

The most useful tool my unconscious has to bring forth its offerings is the journal/notebook. I have kept some version of this for thirty years. In it, I am able to write in a varied and undisciplined way. It requires no skill, unlike writing the poems. In poetry, a deep order exposes the chaos. In the journals, the disorder records patterns and imaginative structures that will later become order.

The pages reproduced here are representative of my notebook that I keep on a weekly—often on a daily—basis. These notebooks were started when I was nine; at that time they were diaries, pure and simple. I kept the gold keys in with a rather large selection of Barbie's shoes. I wrote virtually no journals in high school, but began again in college and continued them quite fervidly while in graduate school, raising a family, working, and writing books of poetry. There are probably a hundred of these journals by now, many sizes, colors, lined and unlined, some with ties, keys, equipped with pressed flowers, diagrams of birds' wings, maps, and ticket stubs. They are—besides family photos—by far my most valued possessions.

I have reproduced a few of these pages once before; otherwise, they haven't been seen by people other than myself. I decided it would be useful to copy a page or two here and there from four or five different notebooks rather than xerox a large "chunk" from one book. That way, you can get an idea of how such a record might be useful for the development of a writing style and for integrating the materials of daily life with philosophical or aesthetic problems a writer might be thinking about. My poems tend to be imagistic and meditative rather than strictly narrative;

Brenda Hillman is an award-winning poet and teaches at Saint Mary's College in Moraga, CA. Her most recent books, both from Wesleyan University Press, are Death Tractates *and* Bright Existence.

thus, when I draft a poem, it often involves the work of pasting together, weaving, assembling lines, ideas, and musical phrases I have collected. These raw materials are almost always recorded first in the journals.

The earliest entry included here is from 1988. I was working hard as a teacher and mother, was in a loving relationship (which was not without problems), and was thinking a lot about gnosticism, inner light, eternal forms, and head lice. The entries from 1990 are concerned with psychological processes around male rage, war, and the suffering body; the reader might note that there are references to Iraq, Christmas shopping, and the junior high school locker on the same page, but certainly that is how this life has been. I worked a lot with trance/hypnosis in a therapeutic situation, which accounts for some of the peculiar references like "the eagle" in these pages. Of the poems produced during this period, some of the ones I printed in *Bright Existence* are "Steinberg Case" and "Autumn Moon."

The "scattery-looking" pages from 1992 I have included because—although they are hard to read—this type of entry is often the most important when I need a breakthrough during a blocked period. (Actually, I don't have many "blocked periods," but, instead, periods when I am writing very far from the center; perhaps this is the form writer's block takes for writers who write a lot but save relatively little. In any case, these periods are painful and frequent.) These entries look as they do because they are written in the middle of the night with the light out. I sleep very lightly, unfortunately, and am often awakened by a dream or a concern or a noise; about ten years ago, I learned that sometimes at night a part of the voice comes through unfiltered, the way it does in hypnosis, and it's a good thing to record these fragments at once when they occur. There are several examples here; one became the opening of a poem called "The Spark."

The longest entry here is from 1993, a partial account of a walk we took on Point Reyes Peninsula. The rest are miscellaneous notes.

I have deleted all the names except for Bob's and Louisa's as it is obvious who they are. In all cases, the entries are continuous, except in a few instances I have deleted material and spliced two pieces together.

The idea of representation
being impossible to give up.
No complacency, though! A
little lizard, then another.
The way back had only
this: a doe came out, then
a fawn, I thought, like me
& Lu. They were frail. They
stared at Bob.

7/2/88

Plums keep falling from the tree —
    a sudden, hard, thump
And across the way, from the little
    gazebo, when I sit, the tiny
    bing-cherry sized ones. It's
an unusually hot day. I went
to sleep early, tired, constipated,
but not unhappy because we'd
had that beautiful walk
    with our parallel thoughts,
and a nice supper.

In the middle of the night (2)
    as usual I woke up. But I

just practically lay there
in anguish, distressed about
my work. Feel like a poker
player with Bob — I don't want
to tell him when it's going
terribly, but when it's going well
I also feel v. superstitious about
talking about it. Anyway, I
lay there. Moonlight streaming
in. The pilot light an all
at once I practically heard
"trapped light" by itself, taken
from bits I had been working
on. It seemed deeply satisfying
and exactly correct, as the
other versions hadn't been. So
what if I'm stealing the title?
I ~~stole~~ transferred the title for 12 dawns
to B. Existence. I felt so
happy. I got up & ~~penned~~
penned much of it ~~in the dark~~,
& woke up excited & still anxious.

(in the future.)

7/12/88

I dreamed ~~was eating~~ was trying to have

thoughts backward. She was sitting at
a table. Every time she would have one
it would appear on the floor as a little
spot, a black spot.

Woke up very weak and out of it.
Had a bad nights with allergies
in Inverness, and last night was
bad too. Not sure why; perhaps
something got to me about what
I was eating. (Kumquats? Black-
berries?) Consequently, feel terrible.
Also feeling very very low
spiritually. I'm not sure why
except there's something I want
to write — before Bright Existence
and the open sequence — feel very
discouraged. I wonder how much of

$\longrightarrow$

Sting on [Charisma] — you have to
have enough confidence to get up
there on ~~stage~~ and create a space
that makes people eager to fill it —
you could do it with silence, though he

creatures, not relating their sex
bings to both sexes. But I also
believe in absolute femininity, tho' not
in its conclusion (service to man).

10/4
Exhausted and depressed this a.m.
Feel I will not be able to write again.
That old, horrible feeling. Have a
headache, feel sickish & discouraged.
Can't even sit up to write too well &
really don't want to — but want this feeling
of just having written something earth shattering.

10/6/88
Still feel miserable about writing but not otherwise.
Bentsen & Quayle debated last night & Bentsen
looked great. Helen started to school with lots
of energy. my classes going well. No problems
except I'm not in the magic. Just need to
work on it. Am so tired of working on things.
Where's my magic save for B? Where's my sustaining
aura? I feel utterly bereft.
        Now its just important to say, Let go, it
will come. Fran & I had a good talk last night
about art. She was great - she reminded me
how Van Gogh did not think once about
immortality but just obsessed because he had
to get one particular yellow that could not
be achieved. That's what I want, that
particular yellow. the protean daily life,

with its shabby little dramas, simply
with not do.

The concept of Alien Life, which the by
aldermess is both suffering &
magisterial.

10/7
The sun is shining weakly outside after
shining all morning. Last night we
went out with Joyce Jenkins and
some writers from the Poets & Writers' excha
program. Barry.

_____

And always this terrible tension between
the daily life & the eternal. Was there
an eternal. Solving that question was all
that mattered. And how terribly oddly
we were placed against it.

I was at the library looking out on some
slightly diseased leaves of some climbing
thing. I was feeling sort of badly because
one of my best students —   — was
upset about his grade. He was displeased
he had gotten a C instead of a B. I felt
terrible talking to him, also terrible tear
this morning I had stopped in and talked
to   about Washboards & she had suggested
that I apply for 5/7ths. time to get
pro-rated salary and I   was standing
5

– The Archers those glittering darts

8/20 Tahoe –

It was co<u>ld</u> last night, cold & rainy. This A.M. clear. B & I made love & we
– felt much better, all doubled back into each other again. That was heaven. Also to sleep 10 hours. Woke up feeling round, organized. It's great. They're gone off to shop.

– The world bent into the wide and the place we slept was with wars ending ~~After an impossible losses~~

Yesterday we stopped at Auburn, at a Foster's Freeze, to get lunch. There were lots of people standing around on the porch of the Foster's Freeze. We decided we would get Beans out because it was so hot in the car. When the people saw the long pink tail everyone vanished to one

side and we got a fine table to ourselves.
So that was a clever thing to do, I
thought.

I think #1 I've only ever had one subject.
About how amazing & upsetting the existence of things
If God's the light was so perfect   is.
Why did things bother to appear.
Tell me that.
The drip of the sap on the sides of the universe.
Why did things arrive.

Maybe there is only one subject.
About how upsetting & amazing the existence is...
That despite the light being perfect
etc..

Walk in desolation Wilderness. Saw
red-breasted nuthatch, several
flycatchers, and — ugh! —
                    sapsucker.

8/21 Tahoe Finally it cleared. Iraq has declared
the 3000 Americans to be hostages.
Bush is golfing. My period is due.

— Second arm of pity

---

had terrible allergies since we
arrived, particularly bad last
night. Couldn't even breathe.

B & I walked our "anniversary
walk" up the Estero. It was a
completely gorgeous day yesterday —
few clouds, light wind. I'm always
cold so I wore a jacket. Up the
Estero trail past the various bare
places into the mixed conifers then
(where we once made love) then
up the trail past the 1st, second, third,
fingers of the estero. Saw many
beautiful birds on the walk, many
egrets, 2 herons, B told a story
about the golden eagle stealing
the chicks of the herons from
Audubon Canyon in its talons, I
Laughed when he said the word talons,
it seemed to come so naturally from within
him whereas I would have had to stay, to
be immoderately literary to come up with it.

Anyway we walked along; when we
came to 2nd arm of Estun we
paused for lunch & looked into the
pond, deeply deeply into the watercress,
and saw to our amazement that
much of what we mistook for
watercress above the surface was
pairs of eyes, frogs' eyes, staring
over at us. There were hundreds
of frogs in the little pond. Bob
spotted a water snake with a red
head dynamically swimming by.
It was a glorious sight but the
most glorious & interesting was the
sight of a frog, very close to
shore, who was turquoise. Brilliant
turquoise. At first I thought it
was some piece of an ancient
carriage that had fallen into the
water. Don't know why I thought
carriage. At 1st just the word
"horse" came to mind. But then
we got closer & realized it was a
big malingering frog of a different

species, its eyes redder, blacker than the others' eyes, which were more amber. I told Bob he looked like an artifact of <u>oxidized copper</u>. (Like from China, c. 2000 B.C.) — I was v. proud of the description, annoyed when B. used it later to some folks on the trail, as if it were his.

We went on up the trail. No wild flowers "to speak of" except monkey flower & some peculiar purplish thing on a stalk. Many strong shrubs seeming to think it was just about spring.

Also a book of poems
called 7<u>th</u> grade —
about <u>that</u> —
• <u>horrible</u> & pleasure

12/8/90 Superintendent Marks resigned
We went & registered at Adams
on the day the superintendent (Marks)
who has built the school up
so much, resigned. Great irony.
We sat in the counsellor's office.
It all felt a little terrifying &
foreign, but I felt confident
in the school when I talked to
the counsellor, Mr. ; who is
highly involved in rescuing
kids from their bad home lives
(he had a group of special boys
who live out in a portable
classroom — Louisa got terrified
at the idea of these kids
being around but was reassured)
Etc. She got registered for stuff she

work on it over the next
few days   Obscure but
deep & clear

Started it. Got thru suffering
i invented shape.

Go to Christ?
Mosaic Christ as title?
or Sorrow of matter?

let Eagle help.

Went running. On the track
I thought of poem abt.
track — in fragments.
W/ wet sweatshirt as a
repeating image.

—The track — wet sweatshirt

doesn't particularly want –
volleyball, etc. But the most
difficult part of the experience
was talking to   ,
                                  , before

we went, who said "Are you
sure you want to do this,
Louisa?" And went on about
how she had not been hearing
anything bad about Portola.
Etc.   . All in all,
It feels painfully like the right
thing for Lu, given the choice,
& given the fact that I can't do
private school at this point; But
so painful to leave that little
place. I dive into the irrational
& the place I. land always
is with some basic fear, that
there will be no there there. Perhaps
we should give up looking for
home & we will be home,

maybe that should be our
main thing in life. Louisa
is too young for that concept.
She's still forming an ego.

Bob & I had our
Friday night tête à tête
& then went to Olivetto — it
was great food but there
was a loudmouth at the next
table who was terrifically intrusive
so they moved us. Chanterelles,
Squab w/ root vegetables.

12/9 Inverness
He was very funny when we
woke up — his eyebrows —
I wrote eyebrowns — like
crickets' dealies & his
jokes — asking if I
wanted him to go into
town to get croissants.
I said I would love to have

a croissant but I didn't
want him to go to the
trouble & he said, it's
all right, it's a "croiss"
I'd gladly bear. Also
he was describing the
style of the guy involved
in the sculpture garden as
an "imitation madcap art
professor."

Driving back fr. Inverness, saw a
deer that had been struck by a
car right here on the Arlington.
It was a large buck, horns
& everything. It was still breathing.
my instinct was to pull over but
we had to go on, Bob was late
for a grad student party. It
Struck me again about the importance
of having an experience while you're
having it. All p. m. we had been
hiking around on the coast trail —

We stopped & saw many birds:
2 kinds of woodpeckers — actually
3, because there were several
flickers, & saw the yellow
bellied Sapsucker again! Studied
some wrens at length & some
dear kinglets. Anyway, I really
felt the need for more meaning —
that it was terrible to have
to rush along & not be able to
go deeply enough. Then when I
saw that deer I felt utterly sad —
this life would vanish there on
the studp stupid urban road
and we would not be there
with it.

The importance of ushering a life out.

Read this w/ yr eyes
closed
little body.
Who almost wasn't.
Read this in the dark
& remember

to Read this in the dark
little are
little body they did not love

Before you there was no time
before you
there was l — the —
Spark
the sexual energy of
the world.

The boys

Read this with your eyes closed
and remember

Read this with your eyes closed
little one -
little body they did not love

So I asked my
love I said
my love ?

so you asked

~~the~~ name is one heaven in

whose fire place

shall I stand

beside

— ~~the~~ Time came first,
but before time was space, and before
space was the sexual energy of the world.

Time came first
but before time was space
and before space
was the sexual energy of the world.

— you who happened only once:

5 |28
— Its so good
that experiences are different.

———

I had a major break through
all a. m. Have been
waiting for the big poem.
Realized my old catacomb
sequence was very good
metaphor for jealousy.
Took it out. Started
re-doing it. Got happy.

immediate:
— finish: female jealousy
     work on Jr. high (8th grade)
     — mending box.
— Chevron poem (Black tankers)
     (seen on hillside)
— female perfection
— time problem.

CHARLES JOHNSON

I started keeping a diary when I was about twelve; my mother suggested the idea. In college the diary transformed itself into a journal in which I wrote poetry, brief essays to myself, and (as with a diary) tried to make sense of daily events. When I started writing fiction, the journal moved more in the direction of being a writing tool. I use cheap spiral notebooks. Into them go notes on everything I experience; I jot down images, phrases used by my friends, fragments of thoughts.... (I now keep an entirely separate journal for recording personal matters.) These writing notebooks sit on my desk fifteen inches deep, along with notebooks I kept from college classes (I save everything, it's shameless...).

When I write, I sit down and let a first draft flow out for as long as inspiration stays with me. I let that first draft be chaotic, if need be: a rush of everything I can feel, imagine, or dredge up. Then I go over it and weed out the junk. Somewhere around the third draft, I begin going through my notebooks hunting for thoughts, images I've had, or ideas about characters (usually observations I make of people around me). Although it takes at least six hours to go back through all these notebooks, I can count on finding some sentence, phrase, or idea I had, say twenty years ago, that is currently useful. I don't carry any of the journals with me—I can't afford to lose them. Instead, I jot notes on whatever is available—hotel stationery, the margins of an old newspaper—and slip it into the notebooks when I get back home.

Charles Johnson is Pollock Professor of Writing at the University of Washington, Seattle; fiction editor of the Seattle Review; *a TV writer/producer; and National Book Award winner for* Middle Passage *(New American Library), to which these notebook excerpts pertain. Next page: a facsimile of the manuscript that became p. 57 of the Plume edition.*

come with the crew.
I want to know what
each man's thinking.

when he Tried pulling it over his enormous head, its collar caught under

his ~~beard~~, leaving him blind for a moment——I believe I could have shot

him then——with both his hands helplessly in the air. "Give me a hand here,

Mr. Calhoun. ~~I~~ *I Trust ye.* I hope ye can see that I need a colored mate to be me

eyes and ears once the Africans are on board." Against my better instincts

to gun him down right there, I helped the Skipper ~~tug~~ *pull* his shirt free, ~~·········~~

~~········· on the side of······~~, tugged off both his steel-reinforced

boots as he pushed me ~~··········~~ from behind. ~~···········~~

open and tell me of any signs of trouble." He ~~···········~~

~~Took a knife to it, then wiped up ········ Turned to the fone Hooks locked his···~~

~~········y· or~~ "Ye'll do that, won't ye"——~~·······~~

~~········~~. Moments later he was asleep, ~~············~~ and I

leaned over him, ~~·················~~

~~·········~~ the crude ring twinned on his left hand and mine, as if, heaven

help me, we were married, and the very thing I'd escaped in New Orleans
unlighted
had, here off the coast of Guinea, overtaken me.

"Be you
Judas?" I
asked. "A Jew?"

P the eyes filled
with hurt·—"Noh"
·· ·······
Sheesh. I need
someone to
keep his
own)

"
Once weekly O'll want a full
report. If there's any To talk, ye'll
Tell me."

made me something of
a betrayer Too.

Poison each man's perception of the
other. By making me the use of each man's
hostile (O had no choice) he subtly
compromised me)
·········· made a ·············
eyes, thinking of ··········, who'd
say these things were said to
tear us.

In a half-sleep he began bellyaching about his
officers, bitterly telling me personal things about
each O never dreamed of and did not wish to know.
He was clearly breaking confidences, betraying
everyone of them in a life so venomous O wanted to
cover my ears. ········, I felt uncomfortable, then
faintly unclean as he described in detail all the dirty
and gossip, weaknesses and shortcomings, for
every mother's son on board. Everyone, it seemed,
had a secret. A shadow, A brutal past or scandalous
That O was nervous Rave the rest of the night. Why was he
saying these things? I could only speculate that something was
seriously wrong with the ship——he never ······ what—— and his
solution was the oldest and simplest in the world. Divide and
Conquer.

Characters

Crew of Republic
Rutherford Calhoun
Capt. Ebenezer Falcon +
Peter Cringle, Mate
Josiah Squibb, Cook
Tommy, cabin-boy
Rev. Meadows
Matthew McIntosh, bratswain. +
Lighthands (boys) +
Ngonyama

Extras
Squibb's parrot
Unga-golahit

New Orleans
Isadora Bailey
Madame Toulouse
Papa Zeringue
Santos

Makanda, Ill.
Jackson Calhoun
Peleg Chandler

Bangalang
Owen Bogha
Ahman-de-bellah

Aquarius
EL
The King

Number of locations = 5
Total characters (named) = 19 *
Number of major characters = 10
  + = died during mutiny.

Chapter Outline

Chap. One —————— The bargain.

Chap. Two ———— Calhoun meets Capt. Falcon and learns that Zeringue has financed this voyage. He learns life at sea, the hardene and hardship, and the crew. He tells story of his brothers.

Chap. Three ———— All mused slaves are taken on board. The revolt. Calhoun is captain by default.

Chap. Four ———— The wandering. He learns of Allmuseri culture. Supplies sd low. Slave die of disease. The ghost ship is following them. They sight land.

Chap. Five ———— Journey to the Dystopia. ⎰ A world
Chap. Six ———— Escape from the Dystopia. ⎱ without black.

Chap. Seven — Back at sea, wandering in space and time.

Chap. Eight — Journey to Dystopia ⎰ A world without whites.
A few of the Allmuseri stay here.

Chap. Nine — At sea again, storms and violent weather, etc.

Chap. Ten — Rutherford boards the Ghost Ship. Sees Capt. Falcon and the dead crew and himself. The magical ship returns him to New Orleans.

Character Note:

Tammy is a Dickensian type orphan. His father died of drink when he was a year old, his mother went insane when he was eight. To avoid the orphanage in New Orleans, he went to sea. Rutherford (and Isadora) will take the ship's boy in — Rutherford is thinking of returning to Makanda, farming, with his new family.

Chapter #8

As R. lies sick, thinking of his decision to marry Isadora (Chap #7), he now has the motivation to ask Meadows why he killed his family. R. is afraid of the responsibility. He wonders if he's up to the requisites Meadows paints for a householder.

Character Note:
Tommy is a Dickensian type orphan. His father died of drink when he was a year old, his mother went insane when he was eight. To avoid the orphanage in New Orleans, he went to sea. Rutherford (and Isadora) will take the ship's boy in—Rutherford is thinking of returning to Makanda, farming, with his new family.
Chapter #8
As R. lies sick, thinking of his decision to marry Isadora (Chap #7), he now has the motivation to ask Meadows why he killed his family. R. is afraid of the responsibility. He wonders if he's up to the requisites Meadows paints for a householder.

139

Note for Sea Story, Chap. One

Isadora explains her virtues to Rutherford, as the old woman in the Chaucer tale does—a monologue of beauty. Once done, she asks him, "Well, what do you have to say?"

I was scared to death.

Sheraton-Palace Hotel

Falcon —

Eating for him was a
Task. He fell to it with a
silent, single-minded
determination, seldom
looking up from the table,
shoveling it down with
efficient, steady forklifts
that favored a man bailing-hay.
In fifteen minutes he was done
and sprang up from the table,
throwing down his wadded up.
(over)

SAN FRANCISCO, CALIFORNIA
415/392-8600

napkin, and was off to
see to some shipboard
chore.

Falcon—
Eating for him was a task. He fell to it with a silent, single-minded determination, seldom looking up from the table, shoveling it down with efficient, steady fork lifts that favored a man bailing hay. In fifteen minutes he was done and sprang up from the table, throwing down his wadded up (over) [on reverse] napkin, and was off to see to some shipboard chore.

The Allmuseri are nominalists,
radical empiricists — each object is
unique for them. They have no universals,
no generic terms. Their language is
impossible to learn. They have, therefore,
no "science." The novel's thematic
tension is between

universals —— vs. —— nominalism
(Zen seeing)

Rutherford's encounter with them
leads to his truly seeing Isolated (and
each person) as a distinct individual
who can be subsumed under no
general categories whatsoever.

The Allmuseri are nominalists, radical empiricists—each object is unique
for them. They have no universals, no generic terms. Their language is
impossible to learn. They have, therefore, no "science." The novel's thematic
tension is between universals—vs.—nominalism (Zen seeing)

Rutherford's encounter with them leads to his truly seeing Isadora (and
each person) as a distinct individual who can be subsumed under no general
categories whatsoever.

Is Ngonyama an outlaw
or criminal among the Allmuseri.
He's been captured with them; he
is responsible for their capture & is
treated badly by them. He knows
English because he is the only one
among them to have contact with whites.

Rutherford learns that Falcon
hates life — he goes to sea precisely
because it is dangerous and he hopes
shipping out will destroy him; he cares
not at all if it destroys his crew,
as well.

Is Ngonyama an outlaw or criminal among the Allmuseri. He's been captured with them; he is responsible for their capture & is treated badly by them. He knows English because he is the only one among them to have contact with whites.

Rutherford learns that Falcon hates life—he goes to sea precisely because it is dangerous and he hopes shipping out will destroy him; he cares not at all if it destroys his crew, as well.

Chapter 6

①. Rutherford is captain. All the duties of the station fall to him; he is responsible for the well-being of 28 other people. Ergo, he experiences a _reversal_ in his life: he goes from being social parasite to _service to others_.

②. Cringle tells his story (biography).

③. Squibb falls sick.

④. Rutherford's remembrances of Isadora.

NOTE

There must be in Cringle's biography a connection foreshadowed for how he turns the Aquarians around.

Chapter 6

1. Rutherford is captain. All the duties of the station fall to him; he is responsible for the well-being of 28 other people. Ergo, he experiences a reversal in his life: he goes from being social parasite to service to others.
2. Cringle tells his story (biography).
3. Squibb falls sick.
4. Rutherford's remembrances of Isadora.
Note
   There must be in Cringle's biography a connection foreshadowed for how he turns the Aquarians around.

Chapter 6 = PACING

1. Cringle and R. discuss being lost. He steps outside Falcon's cabin to look at the stars. Segue into... (2 pages or 3)

2. Insert by Cringle on perception. (½ page) Background on Cringle (1-2 pages)
   — whitespace break —

3. Sighting the ghost ship. Rumors among crew of what it means. (2-3 pages)

4. Diseases spread. Squibb dies. (extend over 5 pages)

5. Looking up from Squibb's body, as Tommy hands him the spy-glass, they see land. (1 page maybe: long paragraph)

Chapter 6: Pacing
1. Cringle and R. discuss being lost. He steps outside Falcon's cabin to look at the stars. Segue into... (2 pages or 3)
2. Insert by Cringle on perception. (½ page) Background on Cringle (1-2 pages)
   —whitespace break—
3. Sighting the ghost ship. Rumors among crew of what it means. (2-3 pages)
4. Diseases spread. Squibb dies. (extend over 5 pages)
5. Looking up from Squibb's body, as Tommy hands him the spy-glass, they see land. (1 page maybe: long paragraph)

Falcon & C. talk.

Intro Allmuseri in general (Don't mention Ngonyama).

C. talks with Meadows. Learns Falcon had a stroke. Also that McIntosh will be Mate, and is training ship's dogs to be killers of slaves.

C. reflects on McIntosh's racism.

Cringle refuses to brand blacks and is demoted.

Ship sets sail.

Squibb seeks his Beloved. What is discover[ed], drawing nearer to her, is that, "I am she." His quest for the Other turns back upon himself, liberating him. Where duality was now there is unity.

Squibb seeks his Beloved. What is discover[ed], drawing nearer to her, is that, "I am she." His quest for the Other turns back upon himself, liberating him. Where duality was now there is unity.

Falcon makes Rutherford promise that he will get him safely back to New Orleans.

Falcon makes Rutherford promise that he will get him safely back to New Orleans.

Jackson Calhoun is spiritual, like the Allmuseri — he carries that African spirituality over into a racist system.

No person, or thing for these Allmuseri could dwell outside the circle of the Whole.

For the Allmuseri, every single human action, situation, and deed is the opportunity to practice sacrifice to their God, was, in fact, their God in action, each tribesman being but a transparency for his unfoldment; each deed to them, therefore, was shot full of spirituality, whether it be signing a treaty with a neighboring tribe or taking a shit. No place was profane. No object divorced from divinity.

Jackson Calhoun is spiritual, like the Allmuseri—he carries that African spirituality over into a racist system.

No person or thing for these Allmuseri could dwell outside the circle of the Whole.

For the Allmuseri, every single human action, situation, and deed is the opportunity to practice sacrifice to their God, was, in fact, their God in action, each tribesman being but a transparency for his unfoldment; each deed to them, therefore, was shot full of spirituality, whether it be signing a treaty with a neighboring tribe or taking a shit. No place was profane. No object divorced from divinity.

149

So it was done; I was the new captain of The Republic. It figured, in a way, that a Negro wouldn't gain control of the steering-wheel until the ship was leaking like a basket, damaged damned near beyond repair, and everyone ready to bail out.

The Allmuseri behead Falcon. Later, when R. sees him on the Phantom ship, his head keeps falling off.

Allmuseri have no fingerprints (identity)

Allmuseri practice—once a week it is their custom to give up a new (or old) desire.

He knew an whole encyclopedia of facts but nary a single truth.

There was — who can doubt it? — magic in this. More importantly, Falcon was rude. And His solution to a dangerous world would use to make himself dangerous.

Tommy = innocent to irony

Cringle = During his childhood. As a child, thought had struck Cringle thunderously, left him frozen, physically immobilized for long whiles and staring into space, his eyes fixed on an idea, a vision so concrete it seemed superimposed upon the spot where he stood. It was a dangerous thing, these visions. In school, friends covered for him; at home it frightened his parents, who feared Peter would hurt himself during these instants of

He had visions to this day, though not so frequently as before.

Falcon = Never having been loved, he settled on being feared

He knew an [sic] whole encyclopedia of facts but nary a single truth.

More importantly, Falcon was rude. And there was—who can doubt it?—magic in this. His solution to a dangerous world was to make himself dangerous.

Tommy: innocent to irony

Cringle: During his childhood, thought struck Cringle thunderously, left him frozen, physically immobilized for long minutes and staring into space, his eyes fixed on'an idea, a vision so concrete it seemed superimposed upon the spot where he stood. It was a dangerous thing, these visions. In school, friends covered for him; at home it frightened his parents, who feared Peter would hurt himself during theses instants of

He had visions to this day, though not so frequently as before.

Falcon: Never having been loved, he settled on being feared

151

MAXINE HONG KINGSTON

*A*t any given time, I have half a dozen notebooks going at once: a couple of daybooks, some workbooks for my "novel," two sketchbooks—one of dreams and one of summers at the Grand Canyon—a diary of the coming day, and this "Notes Toward Poems."

I have learned that dreams are more accurately set down in drawings (with color pens if dreaming in color) than in words. I divide the page into three sections because dreams are often in three acts, and do have beginning-middle-end. You can get at a dream by drawing a triptych. When you put dreams into words, you bring them into the reasoning logical world. I used to write my dreams; now I only draw them.

During the summers, I live at the Grand Canyon with my husband, Earll Kingston, who does a one-man John Wesley Powell show. Speechless before the canyon, I sketch it. No matter how large the canvas, a picture of the canyon is miniature. So, I've been drawing it on extra-small pages, which I use as postcards to friends. I've also given up coloring my Grand Canyons, and draw in pencil and ink. Gray graphite and black lines in fine-nib pen and ink represent billions of years of silence. Down inside the silent canyon, I know that much of what I thought to be the world's noise is the roaring and chattering of my own mind. (Europeans will stop and want to look at my drawing and talk to me about what I'm doing; Japanese will themselves be sketching; Americans will refuse eye contact and point their videocam at the section of the canyon I'm facing.) In words, here are the few thoughts I've had regarding the canyon: If we human beings were to make our species extinct, the Grand Canyon, from which uranium was once

Maxine Hong Kingston teaches at the University of California, Berkeley. She is the author of The Woman Warrior *(Knopf), winner of the National Book Critics Circle Award for Non-Fiction. Her first novel,* Tripmaster Monkey— His Fake Book, *was published by Knopf. The drawing on the next page was sent as a postcard, dated 18 July 1992, to Judy Foosaner, an artist who lives in Point Richmond, CA.*

mined, would still be here almost exactly as I see it at this moment. I like resting, not enwording, contemplating things rather than people. Most people dream heavily while sleeping near or in the Grand Canyon; dreams seem to come out of that great hole. I put the drawings of those dreams in the Grand Canyon notebook rather than the dream notebook.

The diary of the coming day and the "Notes Toward Poems" are genres I invented last year. The first writing of the morning: I imagine the day I want to live. I'm hoping that then I can make real the day I've written. Ideally, I write "Notes Toward Poems" in the afternoon, the middle of the day. I sit on the tatami floor and write at the low bamboo table, the only piece of furniture in the room. I recollect and note poetic states, for which I don't have all the poetic words yet. Please note that the old age I'm writing about is not my old age but my mother's. I am trying to bear my mother growing very old. She is about to be ninety years old. I was fifty-two on 27 October 1992, the day I started the poem notebook.

I hardly ever re-read these notebooks, nor find a use for them: I am joyful and free.

Thought about 3:15 a.m. Oct. 27, 1992
written afternoon next day —
  in the Japanese room

The street corner orderly
the lines, trees as is —
just right.

The dawn took forever
until I learned it
was the middle of the night
And I was wide-awake
jet lagged.

Dark with ~~street lights~~ —
still — no traffic and
no people
Respite — the exact
present moment —
The way the light falls
is perfect

1

November 20, 1992

I forgot. I forgot my poetry & my resolve — until I saw this book, and remembered only — there was something important I had begun. How easy it is to forget poetry.

I was going to think about the filing cabinets — the index card library cabinets that the antique shop had gotten from Mills College after they'd computerized. And what if I bought a bank of them

2

what would I put in them / in the
drawers? Things / Stuff
Collections

jewels	dried flowers & leaves	rocks	Photos	burned things
make-up	Postcards from friends	Postcards I paint	pens	little soaps
matches	Keys	Candles	Pencils	tea
red paper	envelopes	Post-Its	Calling cards	inks
eye glasses	magnifying glasses	sewing kit	small toys	Chopsticks
Matches	Anessich	Wint-o-Greens	Spindles	Chops
Candles				

3

Mom walked for Dr. Aziz —
"See how fast I can go. Are
you watching? Is he
watching?" She kept looking
over her shoulder to see
whether the handsome
Indian doctor was
watching.

Sunday

Nights ago, maybe after reading
MFK Fisher's "Tally," I let come in
whatever may be out there toward
the left. I saw (again) the rounded
helmets — There's not one but many
people/spirits out there always —
whom I worry about, + they are
haunting/watching over/waiting for
me. They are combat soldiers. +
they are real to other people too —
like the Night Watcher/Warriors
that walk on the water + also
go thru the streets in Hawaii.

My black Nicaraguan uncle
my mother's "little brother"
in a fit because no one helps him
everybody left for the Americas
+ does not send money [my mother
withholding the thousand I gave
her, which is bothering her
conscience whether she feels
physically good or bad] —
and his son got bitten by the
snake in the next commune that
was none of his business but he
went to the rescue ——— + his
other son went mad after they
arranged a wedding for Saturday
"you're going to get married on
Saturday" to a woman he'd
never seen before ——— this
uncle dug up the graves + scattered
the bones of his parents — my grandfather
+ grandmother — + wrote to everybody
to tell us.

Dec. 3, 1992

The frailty of old age — no, not just frailty but the quick changes — one moment practically dead, & the next supernaturally strong — cooking a turkey, painting the floor, locked out all night — So the way an old person plans is that at the last moment, she can decide to stay home, not go to the party, not keep the appointment. You do what you feel like when the moment comes. You know what you feel at the moment.
I have been trying to live like that. I go less crazy if I let myself not go through w/things at the last moment.

Nothing / Empty / Void

There are no tasks. I don't have to do anything. I don't need the money, & I don't need the exercise / aggravation. I am of an age — I've learned, read, made money, made a career, met many, many people. I may do not even need to write a next book. I've raised a kid. I don't need any more dresses, houses, cars, things. [Except for the big deed / dream — to make a peaceful world?] Places — I've been to all the places I need to go to. The appointments & projects are just to make life interesting.

what happens when you don't
panic to fill in the time?

That tremble on the
wire — no use,
& free

Dec. 6 —

Suddenly free from the life
that my parents had me
for the purpose of Torturing
me.

How did I become convinced
of such a craziness?

And how did I get free?

Sunday —
I shall spend this day
doing whatever I want
moment to moment.
    Bake cookies, shortbread.
    Weed the peas coming up.
    Write when + where I
            please
    Look for gifts for Katie + Li.
        Like Pena, you look
    about the house for your
    own things to give away.
    Even after the fire, I
        have things to give
            away.

    I like wrapping gifts.

Dec 7

During the year after the
fire, I watched Star
Trek a lot — it fell at
the right times. One
night, there was all night
Star Trek — 7:00 the
old "Star Trek"; then "The
Next Generation," then
Star Trek Movie, Then
another old, old Star Trek.
I liked the order, the calm
sitting at the computers;
the orderly dress, the simple
commands from the captain.

15 February —

After reading T. C. Boyle's "Filthy
With Things" —— what
30/60 items I would
⌐as a couple
bring back —

1. my mss.

2. a piece of jewelry —
which one? ⌐ the jade heart
[Process — think of one
per day]

3. a first edition Woman Warrior

DORIANNE LAUX

I've kept a journal since I was around twelve years old. For many years the entries were personal, filled with daily events, adolescent feelings and musings, and, on occasion, a poem or an idea for a poem. About ten years ago my first poetry teacher, Steve Kowit, asked me if I'd been writing any poems lately. I said, "No, I'd only been writing in my journal." His response was, "Jesus, don't waste your time writing about your life. Who cares about that? Write poems." It was useful advice. The next day, rather than making the typical journal entry, I wrote about my day "creatively," trying to capture the most significant events in poetic form. It helped. I found myself writing many more poems.

The entries here are taken, somewhat randomly, from journals dating back to 1987. Often I would give myself the task of merely writing a prescribed number of lines, seventeen, for instance. Sometimes, when I couldn't write, I doodled. Other times I simply jotted down ideas, passing thoughts, an image, a dream. It's quite embarrassing to read over what you've written in a journal; even when it's not particularly personal, it *feels* quite personal, if only because it hasn't yet reached the printed page. And also, for me, there is the further embarrassment of spelling, grammar, and punctuation, which are not high priorities when I'm journal writing.

I have no idea of the usefulness of these scribblings to others. I know journal writing works for me in the sense that on a daily basis I am taking what happens in my head, running it down through my heart, then up through my shoulder, down my arm, and into my fingers that hold the pen. I like the physicality of writing by hand, the act of translating what I'm feeling and thinking into words on a page. Writing daily, or almost daily, no matter what comes out, makes me feel whole, purposeful, balanced, scrubbed clean. There is so much about the process of writing that is mysterious to me, but this is one thing I've found to be true: Writing begets writing.

Dorianne Laux teaches at the University of Oregon, Eugene. Her most recent book is What We Carry *(BOA Editions, Ltd.).*

12·5·92

Bessie Smith singing Georgia on my mind —
Night settling in over the rooftops —
An attic room, the walls slanting into ceiling.
Two overnight bags next to each other on
the sink, close, but not touching.
Piano trills + rain on the roof.
Eighteen lines to go.
No, Seventeen... And soon. Mia Farrow
in the Great Gatsby, her face framed
in pearls, Robert Redford, sinking
in the swimming pool. Pink water.
Covering the rose petals — 40 on one rose
alone. Nothing more important to do
40 years old. 50 years old. 16 years old
A chair by the open window. A note.
The grapevines in December — rows of
red leaves. 3 peacocks. 3 vultures.
3 peacocks on the road. 3 vultures in
a tree. 50/50. That's Life.
Lady Di + her sad eyes. Daisy Buchanan.
If men lead lives of quiet desperation
women lead lives of mute desperation.
Mute. No sound at all. One line to go.
Bessie alive again. Impossible.

I have always loved the world,
in spite of itself, the chancreous
volcanos, the ~~eye~~ lurid eye
of the Iguana, the lure
of black water. I guess
because it gives ~~back~~,
what it takes, manure to
flower, dead wood
to mushroom, water
to rain. Even when the worst
was upon me, the father's
belly large with his childrens
souls, even as the light was sucked
from my mouth, my eyes
darkening, even then,
I watched the ~~spider~~ fly climb
the wall, iridescent, winged,
a holy image to carry
with me until I woke.

11/19

I'm writing w/ Ava's pen, the one she marked AVA in red letters in two places, the shaft & the cap, then taped it so no one would take it from her desk, as Ron must have, slipped it in his coat pocket without a thought — and when I clean the house after a year, I find it, Ava's pen, & write my one hour with it adding insult to injury. But it's ava's pen, so I'm not responsible for what comes out, I can say anything; sky on fire in the rain, screech of car tires, then the silence, then the crash, dirt in the furnace, cat wet & dying on the couch. Ava's boyfriend, dead of cancer, is watching me, watching how I use

what's been taken, though
I know it's only been
misplaced — Ava thinks
her boyfriend's been taken,
but he must feel
misplaced, climbing
though the clouds
endlessly toward her,

Rare books, no ones reading them, don't give the public what it wants, force on them what they don't want —

Dead bird on the lawn — dog & cat looking at it.

The clouds are dragging their shadows across the hills —
The high tension power lines turn their silver skeletons toward the sun, then disappear into the grey shade

I'll Be Seeing You   Jack Yellen
Aint She Sweet
Happy Days are Here Again

Hearts & names on the dusty windsheild, finger in the dust American Flags bumper stickers, decals, taped to the windsheild San Onofre, San Clemente, Casa de Oro.

Give me the beat boys & free m'
soul   wanta get lost in your
Rock & Roll & drift away — Take me

O the bright hair, glistening in sweat
the mouth   stick in sex
the hands   rough and struck
dumb   to the touch
of nipple   & cut, bright
slit   the fingers slip
into   then lift
to the lips   the quick tongue
sucked   to the root,
the eyes   that slay;
the long, unbroken cries
of birds, the intake of breath,
the white, white
            spilling

The halo that follows

Mothers of the ~~mind~~
the psyche
untwist and ~~may~~ reshape
souls

We're dying Steven, we're all
dying, Every minute we
have one less minute to live

. Pricilla worked like a
broken machine, stiff
with a few cogs missing

sidereal day - successive
transits of a star or of the
vernal equinox - solar day,
lunar day

day bill
day blush
day eyed
day gang

evening - dusk comes after twil.
morning - dusk comes before twil
dusk is darker than twil.

dawn
sunrise

dusk
dusk

twilite

dark

daylight
sunrise   sunset
                 dusk
twilit   twilight
deesk   twilit
                 dusk

night

Martin Cruz Smith

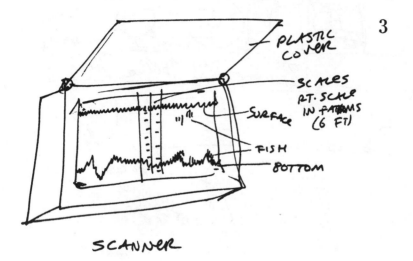

3

PLASTIC COVER

SCALES
RT. SCALE
IN FATHOMS
(6 FT)

SURFACE

FISH

BOTTOM

SCANNER

OTHER BOATS USED NEWER TV COLOR MONITORS

Martin Cruz Smith lives in Mill Valley, CA. He is the author of Gorky Park *and* Red Square *(both Random House). This is a facsimile of a journal he kept while doing research for his second novel,* Polar Star *(Random House). He used only the right-hand pages, thus the odd numbers printed in the upper right corner.*

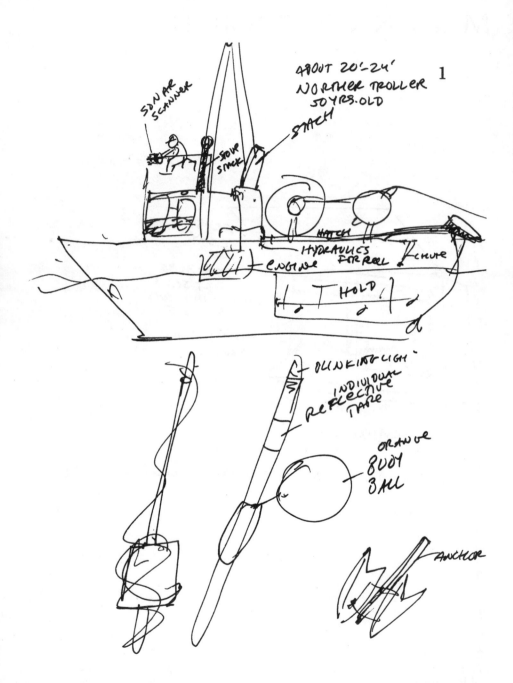

5

PAUL WOODS, HIS DECKHAND JOHN & I SET OUT FROM MARSHALL BOATYARD ABOUT 4:45 PM TO SCAN TOMALES BAY BEFORE SUNSET AT 5:21, WHEN THE FISHERMEN ARE ALLOWED TO SET THEIR NETS. PAUL, A FORMER MINISTER & PEACE CORPS VOLUNTEER, IS KNOWN AS 'DIGGER' OR 'DIG' AROUND THE BOATYARD. HE'S BEEN A COMMERCIAL FISHERMAN ABOUT 10 YRS. AND HAS FISHED HERRING, SALMON & CRAB. INSIDE THE BAY & OUT ON THE OCEAN. THIS IS HIS LAST SEASON. HE'S SELLING HIS BOAT, THE 'EVA U', AND SO KEEPS SOME SLIGHTLY OUDATED EQUIPMENT ON HER, LIKE HER FISH SCANNER, REPLACED ON OTHER BOATS BY COLOR TV MONITORS.

THE SEASONS HAVE BEEN BAD AND HE IS BITTER ABOUT GOV'T REGULATION. A HUGE TUNA FLEET USED TO OPERATE LOCALLY. THE FLEET WOULD RANGE FROM ALASKA TO BAJA CALIFORNIA. THEN THE GOV'T SAID THAT THE FISHERMAN WERE NOT ALLOWED TO CATCH, HOWEVER ACCIDENTALLY, PORPOISE. FOREIGN BOATS IN AMERICAN WATERS COULD CATCH PORPOISE, BUT NOT AMERICAN BOATS. A CALIFORNIA FISHERMAN DEVISED A NET THAT WOULD AUTOMATICALLY FREE ALMOST EVERY PORPOISE CAUGHT, BUT THE GOV'T SAID 'NO, EVERY PORPOISE.' DURING THE

CONTROVERSY, THE FISHERMAN'S SON ~~XXXXXX~~ WENT
INTO THE WATER TO FREE A PORPOISE IN THE NET.
THE OLD MAN WATCHED HIS SON BEING EATEN BY
SHARKS. THE MAIN RESULT OF THE RULING WAS
THAT THE AMERICAN FLEET DISAPPEARED, THEN
REAPPEARED AS A MEXICAN ~~FLEET~~ OPERATING FROM
JUST SOUTH OF THE BORDER.

THE BAY IS TIGHTLY REGULATED. YOU HAVE
AN INSIDE-THE-BAY PERMIT OR AN OUTSIDE-THE-BAY
PERMIT. YOU HAVE PERMITS FOR SEPERATE SEASONS
& QUOTAS ~~XXXXXXXXXX~~ THAT LIMIT YOUR CATCH.
WEEKENDS, THE BAY IS RESERVED FOR RECREAT-
IONAL USE, THOUGH THE BOATS SOMETIMES JUST
GO OUT & SCAN.

BECAUSE THEY ARE ABOUT TO HAUL HERRING,—
THEY HOPE—THE FISHERMEN WEAR CLOTHING
COMMITTED TO FISHING. 'CAT' CAPS, WINDBREAKERS
& SWEATSHIRTS THAT WILL GO UNDER SLICKERS,
RUBBER PANTS, HIGH BOOTS. ONE IS A LAWYER, &
'FAT ~~STAN~~' IN A SCRAGGLY BEARD, WHO REVELS IN A
BOAT FAMOUS FOR THE FILTH & DEBRIS OF HIS
CABIN. MIKE GOLD IS FROM NEW YORK. HIS CREW
IS 2 YOUNG WOMEN CALLED 'THE GOLDETTES.' IN
GENERAL, THE OLDER MEN LOOK LIKE ~~FARMERS~~; THE
YOUNGER MEN LOOK LIKE THE SORT ~~WHO~~ WHO HANG
AROUND FILLING STATIONS.

JOHN IS SHORT, WHISKERY, BEAT-UP ~~XXXXX~~
FOR HIS AGE, WHICH IS PROBABLY YOUNG 30'S. HE

HAS HIS OWN BOAT + FISHED TOMALES BAY FOR 8 YRS., BUT DOESN'T HAVE A PERMIT. HE FIGURES THERE ARE 100 GUYS WAITING FOR THE NEXT PERMIT.

ONE VIETNAMESE FAMILY HAS A BOAT.

ON THE DOCK THERE IS A SENSE OF GROWING ANTICIPATION. THE FRIENDLY PEOPLE GET MORE FRIENDLY, BORROWING SOLDER, SUGGESTING IN A GENTLE WAY THEY MIGHT WANT TO EASE THEIR BOAT THROUGH, + THE GLUM ONES SEEM MORE GLUM. THE SEASON HAS BEEN BAD <u>AND</u> ODD. USUALLY, A CATCH IS ~~BIG~~ ALL OR NOTHING. FOR WEEKS IN TOMALES BAY THE CATCH HAS BEEN A STEADY, MISERABLE DRIBBLE OF FISH. TONIGHT, HOWEVER, THE NEWS IS THAT 3 MAJOR SCHOOLS OF HERRING ~~ARE~~ ^{ARE} ABOUT TO ENTER OR ALREADY ^{ARE} ~~NOW~~ IN THE BAY.

~~THEY'RE TALK OF TO YRS OLD WHEN THE FIRST GENERATED TOMALES BAY + PEOPLE SAID A BOAT SO BIG COULD~~

THE 'EVA V' IS A DOUBLE-ENDER NORTHERN TROLLER ABOUT 50 YRS. OLD. SHE'S APP. 20-25' ~~LONG~~ LONG + SHE WAS THE BIGGEST COMMERCIAL BOAT IN THE BAY MANY YEARS AGO. NOW SHE'S ONE OF THE SMALLER BOATS, ~~W~~ <u>W</u> A TINY CABIN + A NARROW BEAM. 'DOUBLE-ENDER' MEANS HER WHOLE HOLD PRACTICALLY FILLS UP IF YOU WANT TO JUMP THRU THE HATCH + STUFF FISH INTO

COMPARTMENTS FORWARD ON EITHER SIDE OF THE ENGINE. SHE HOLDS, STUFFED, 6 TONS. A MODERN 'BACK LOADER' LOADS MORE QUICKLY &, WITH A BROADER BEAM, HOLDS AS MUCH OR MORE. BUT PAUL THINKS THERE IS ALSO AN ADVANTAGE TO BEING A SMALL, QUICK BOAT IN THE BAY & THE 'EVA U' IS THAT.

WE ARE ONE OF THE LAST BOATS TO ENTER THE BAY THIS EVENING. THE WATER IS CHOPPY, THE WIND IS BRISK. I AM IN LONG JOHNS, SHIRT, LEATHER JACKET, SLICKER, PANTS, LONG RUBBER BOOTS + CAP + I AM ALREADY COLD. JOHN GOES UNDER + STARTS THE STOVE. COFFEE ESTABLISHES ITSELF EARLY AS A LEITMOTIF IN JOHN'S LIFE. MAYBE IT'S A DECKHAND'S RESPONSIBILITY, WARMING UP STALE PASTRIES + PUTTING ON WATER FOR INSTANT COFFEE, BUT JOHN THROWS HIMSELF INTO IT. ALL WE HEAR FROM THE WARM GALLEY IS A QUESTION ABOUT THE STOVE'S SMOKESTACK, WHETHER ITS LOUVERED TOP IS SPINNING. WE SPIN IT.

THERE ARE CLOSE TO 40 COMMERCIAL FISHING BOATS IN THE WATER BY 5:21.

13

THE BRIDGE OF THE 'EVA U' IS SET OUT THUS:

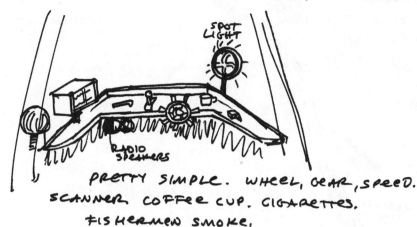

PRETTY SIMPLE. WHEEL, GEAR, SPEED.
SCANNER, COFFEE CUP. CIGARETTES.
FISHERMEN SMOKE.

THE MARKS ON THE SCANNER WERE
FEEBLE. PAUL WAS RELUCTANT TO SET HIS
NETS; SOMETIMES HE'S THE LAST ONE TO SET.

TOO HIGH, BECAUSE
NETS SINK TO BOTTOM

TOO
NARROW

TOO LITTLE

DIFFERENT FISHERMEN HAVE DIFFERENT STYLES.
SOME WANT TO SET ALL AROUND ONE AREA, OTHERS
BACK & FORTH

THE BOTTOM READING VARIES BECAUSE WE
ARE PASSING DIRECTLY OVER THE SAN ANDREAS
FAULT. TOMALES BAY IS THE SAN ANDREAS
FAULT.

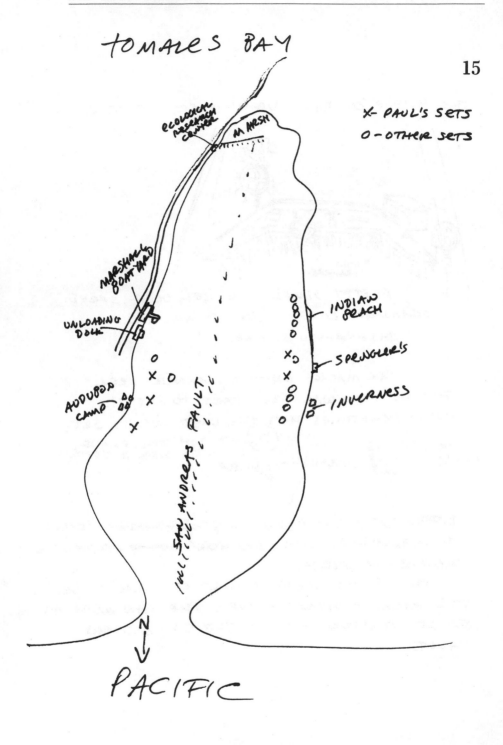

ACCORDING TO BIOLOGISTS, HERRING ONLY SPAWN ON eel GRASS. FISHERMEN SAY THE FISH WILL SPAWN ON ANYTHING, BUT THERE'S NO DOUBT THAT THE 'BEST SET' IS THE NET CLOSEST TO THE BEACH, AN 'INSIDE SET.'

INSIDE

OUTSIDE

It's ALSO WHERE THOSE HERRING W THE HIGHEST PERCENTAGE OF ROE ARE FOUND. THE FACT IS THAT WE ARE CATCHING ROE, NOT FISH. THE ROE IS A JAPANESE DELICACY + YOU ARE PAID NOT ONLY FOR HOW MUCH FISH YOU CATCH BUT ON A SCALE DETERMINED BY THE ROE COUNT. ON THE AVERAGE, SAY, $1,000 PER 1,000 lbs. FOR A 10% COUNT; $1,300 PER 1,000 lbs. FOR A 13% COUNT. LESS THAN 10%, YOU MIGHT GET $100 FOR 1,000 lbs. TAKE IT OR LEAVE IT. BUT THERE WOULDN'T BE A HERRING SEASON IN TOMALES BAY WITHOUT JAPAN.

FINALLY, <u>W</u> POOR MARKS ON THE SCANNER,
PAUL SET THE NET. ACTUALLY, JOHN SET IT.

PAUL SLOWED THE ENGINE AND SHOUTED
'STAND BY!'
'STANDING BY!' JOHN ANSWERED AND
STOOD AT THE STERN <u>W</u> A LIGHT & BUOY.

ANCHOR

'DRAG IT!', PAUL SHOUTED.
JOHN THREW THE LIGHT & BUOY OVER.

LIGHT

GREEN REFLECTIVE TAPE
(PAUL'S ID)

'DRAGGING!'
'STAND BY <u>W</u> ANCHOR!,' PAUL SHOUTED.
JOHN ATTACHED THE ANCHOR TO A RING IN THE
UNREELING ROPE.
'STANDING BY!'

21

'THROW THE ANCHOR!'
'ANCHOR OVER!'
PAUL CAREFULLY MOVED FORWARD, LETTING THE
ANCHOR DRAG OUT THE NET. IT'S A GILL NET

2" ACROSS WHEN PULLED SO!

AS THE NET UNREELS THE REEL ITSELF
SPINS FASTER & FASTER, SOMETIMES TOO
FAST FOR JOHN TO MAKE SURE IT ISN'T
CATCHING IN ITSELF & DOUBLING UP ON THE
REEL. THEN HE SHOUTS 'BACKLASH!' & PAUL
HAS TO STOP THE BOAT UNTIL JOHN UNTANGLES
THE NET. ONE DIFFICULTY IS THAT JOHN HAS
TO WORK OVER THE 'SHAKER'. THE NET IS
NOT NEAT, IT'S A MESS.

REEL   SHAKER

AT THE END OF THE NET, JOHN ATTACHES
ANOTHER ANCHOR & LIGHT & BUOY & FREES
THE NET & THE NET IS SET.

PAUL HAS 2 NETS ON THE REEL, SO HE IMMEDIATELY CHARGES AHEAD + SCANS THE BOTTOM. TONIGHT THERE IS A NORTHWEST WIND + A HALF MOON. 'THEY SAY, NO HERRING ON A NORTHWIND AND NO MERRING ON A HALFMOON,' PAUL SAYS. 'THEY ALSO SAY, ALWAYS HERRING ON A NORTHWIND + ALWAYS HERRING ON A HALFMOON. A MAN WROTE A BOOK CALLED 'KNOWN FACTS ABOUT HERRING. HE PUT IT ALL IN.'

IT'S A CLOUDY EARLY EVENING. WHEN GULLS MILL AROUND LIKE THIS   PAUL SAYS IT'S A STORM SIGN. THESE   ARE SMALL GULLS. PAUL JUST CALLS   THEM 'SPAWN BIRDS' BECAUSE THEY, + SOME OTHER BIRDS, EAT ANY ROE THAT FLOATS TO THE SURFACE.

SEA LIONS ARE ALSO OUT HUNTING FISH. THEIR DOG HEADS BOB ALONG, SEEMINGLY IGNORING THE BOATS, THEN THE SLEEK BODY TWISTS + GOES UNDER.

MOST OF THE BOATS SET THEIR NETS ALONG THE ~~NATURAL~~ WESTERN BEACH. PAUL IS UNIMPRESSED, THO HE SEES 'HIGH LINERS' AMONG THEM. 'HIGH LINERS' ARE FISHERMEN W THE BIGGEST CATCHES. HE HAS BEEN A 'HIGH LINER'. NOT LATELY.

WITH 2 NETS TO SET, YOU PLAY A SORT OF
LEAPFROG. SET 'A', SCAN, SET 'B', SCAN, PICK 'A',
SCAN, SET 'A' SCAN, AND ON, TRYING TO THINK TWO
MOVES AHEAD, KEEPING IN MIND THAT THE MARKS
YOU SEE ON THE SCANNER ARE FISH THAT ARE
MOVING. THEY'LL BE COMING IN ON THE TIDE, THEN
GOING OUT ON IT AFTER MIDNIGHT. ALSO, THEY'LL TEND
TO MOVE TOWARD THE BEACH. WITH CLOSE TO 40 BOATS
SCANNING, SETTING + PICKING, THE BAY CAN BE
ACTIVE.

AFTER SETTING THE SECOND NET ON SLIGHTLY
BETTER MARKS, WE RETURN TO PICK THE FIRST.

JOHN
STARTS
HYDRAULICS
+ PUTS
REEL INTO
GEAR.

JOHN PULLS IN THE LIGHT + BUOY W A GAFF. PAUL
HAS PUT THE BOAT IN NEUTRAL AT THAT END OF THE
NET WHERE HE WILL NOT DRIFT INTO, IN OTHER WORDS,
AWAY FROM THE TIDE. ONCE JOHN PULLS IN THE ANCHOR
PAUL CLIMBS DOWN FROM THE BRIDGE + STARTS THE
SHAKER. THERE ARE A FEW FISH IN THE NET, 8-10", SILVERY
W BLACK-RINGED EYES, CAUGHT BY THEIR GILLS ON THE
MONOFILAMENT.

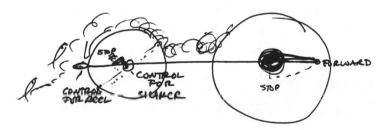

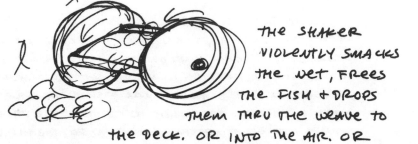

THE SHAKER VIOLENTLY SMACKS THE NET, FREES THE FISH + DROPS THEM THRU THE WEAVE TO THE DECK. OR INTO THE AIR. OR BREAKS THEM IN HALF. THE SHAKER IS A NEW DEVICE + A GODSEND TO FISHERMEN. BEFORE, THEY HAD TO SHAKE THE NET MANUALLY, REQUIRING ANOTHER DECKHAND + NETS ON THE GUNWALES TO CATCH THE FLYING FISH. EVEN SO, THEY THREW A LOT OF FISH BACK IN THE WATER.

THE CATCH IS 250 lbs. NOT MUCH. NOT NOTHING.

WITH A SCREWDRIVER, JOHN PICKS UP THE LID OF THE STOW HOLE + RICKS + SHOVELS + PUSHES THE FISH DOWN INTO THE HOLD. PAUL RETURNS TO THE BRIDGE. JOHN HOSES DOWN THE DECK W A HOSE THAT IS ALWAYS KEPT RUNNING + USUALLY TRAILS IN THE WATER. THE LID IS SLIPPED BACK ON THE STOWHOLE; NO ONE WANTS TO BREAK A LEG.

29

'THESE MARKS ARE DANDY!' PAUL SHOUTS. DANDY IS THE
GOOD SIDE OF THE SPECTRUM, THE DIFFERENCE BETWEEN
JUST GOOD & GREAT BEING THE EMPHASIS ON 'DANDY!'
THOSE MARKS, THE THIRD SET, IS THE FIRST BIG HAUL,
CLOSE TO 800 lbs. (EVERYTHING IS ESTIMATE). THE
HERRING PLAIN DECORATE THE NET. A STRONG OVERHEAD
DECK LIGHT IS USED WHEN REELING IN, & AS THE FISH
SHAKE OUT OF THE NET THEIR SCALES FLY LIKE
SILVER EMBERS. 'THAT'S A LOG OF FISH.' 'THAT'S A
STREAM.' 'YOU CAN WALK ON THESE.' 'THESE FISH
ARE CEMENT.' THIS IS IT, THE FIRST REAL RUN OF
THE WHOLE HERRING SEASON. TONIGHT IS THE NIGHT.

ON THE BRIDGE THE RADIO IS CRACKLING AS
FISHERMEN CALL FRIENDS AT HOME. 'COME ON RIGHT
ACROSS TO INDIAN BEACH.' CONVERSATIONS ARE SHORT.
'SEE YOU AT THE DOCK.' A LOT OF THESE MEN MUST LIVE
RIGHT ON THE BAY.
IN THE WATER, FRIENDS SLOW TO SHOUT WHERE THE
BEST MARKS ARE. 'THEY'RE THICK AS HORSESHIT OVER
THERE.'
AT THE SAME IT'S SERIOUS & COMPETITIVE. GET THE
BEST MARK, GET THE BEST SET, PICK THE NET FIRST
& SET IT AGAIN. THESE MEN ARE QUITE LITERALLY
HAULING IN MONEY, PULLING IN SILVER. NETS ARE
STRUNG EVERYWHERE AND AS BOATS CHARGE BACK &
FORTH THE FIRST ACCIDENTS ARE HEARD. IF YOU RUN
OVER A NET & FOUL IT, IT WILL TAKE 90 MINUTES

FOR THE DIVER TO COME FROM THE DOCK, DIVE IN THE WATER & FREE THE NET FROM THE SCREWS. THEN THE NET MUST BE MENDED. 2-3 HOURS CAN BE LOST DURING THE SHORT, PRECIOUS RUN. THAT'S ONE REASON WHY PAUL SETS APART FROM THE CONCENTRATION OF OTHER SETS. JOHN REALLY WANTS TO STAY AWAY FROM OTHER BOATS; HE'S THE MAIN MENDER.

CLOUDS HAVE CLEARED. IT'S A BRIGHT, HALF-MOONLIT NIGHT. SEA LIONS PERFORM ACROBATICS COMING UP & DOWN FOR HERRING. THE BOATS LOOK LIKE MAGICAL

CARAVALS IN THE DARK. UNLESS THEY'RE PICKING A NET & SHAKING HERRING. THEN THEY ARE

STAGE LIT CHARACTERS WORKING SOME STRANGE WATER-BORN LOOM.

PAUL SAYS 'THIS IS HOW GOD INTENDED FISHING TO BE.'

33

We are awash in herring, we are up to our knees in herring. Herring is rising up to the gunwales & already covers the little poop deck. John pulls in the anchor & light. Paul is already on the bridge & swinging the boat toward marks he saw when we came to pick. 'Stand by!' No time to put the fish in the hold. John kicks enough fish off the poop deck so he move at least. 'Drag it!' 'Anchor!' As soon as the net is set a John & I squeeze 1,000 lbs. of herring through a 10" stow hole. To do in us, John has to go on his hands & knees, has to practically submerge himself in the herring on the deck to even locate the hole, then pry up the lid. Immediately, the fish start swirling down it like water. Not fast enough. There's a shovel. The shovel's not fast enough. We are both on our hands & knees, on our stomachs, herding fish toward the hole. The deck is left coated in scales, slimey milt, roe. Hose down. 'Stand by!' You can't move fast enough. John, who had seemed phlegmatic, is now a demon. No matter how fast I move, he moves faster & it comes to me: This son of a bitch is working for money.

THE MOON IS GONE. WE SEEM TO BE WORKING A COLD FURNACE. SCALES HAVE COLLECTED IN GOBS OF SILVER FROM OUR BOOTS UP TO OUR COLLARS. THE SHAKER & NET ARE NO RESPECTERS OF FISH. THERE IS NOT MUCH FLOPPING ON THE DECK. THESE FISH ARE 99% DEAD & SCRAPED & SOMETIMES CUT IN HALF. THE ONES THAT REACH THE REEL BECOME BOUND LIKE FLIES BEING ROLLED IN A WEB.

PAUL IS PROUD OF HIS HOME-MADE SHAKER, A VERSION OF A DEVICE EVERY BOAT BUT ONE CARRIES. WE SEE THAT BOAT, ITS SIDE NETS UP, THE MEN SHAKING THE NET BY HAND LIKE MEN TOSSING COINS IN A BLANKET. A DANGER OF SHAKING BY HAND IS THAT, GETTING HIT ~~IN THE~~ ~~EYE~~ BY A FISH. PAUL ~~HAS~~ SUFFERED A DETACHED RETINA THAT WAY LAST YEAR. AFTER THE SECOND NET, I PUT MY GLASSES. ON THE THIRD NET I CAUGHT A FISH RIGHT IN THE LENSES.

THE BOAT IS LISTING FROM THE FISH BADLY LOADED IN THE HULL. JOHN HAS TO GO THROUGH THE HATCH & PUSH THEM AROUND. WE SEE A BOAT GO BY, ITS STERN ALMOST UNDER-WATER. I ASK, HALF-HUMOROUSLY, WHETHER BOATS EVER OVERLOAD & SINK. YEAH, SAYS PAUL. ONE LAST YEAR. IT IS A ~~FRENZY~~.

37

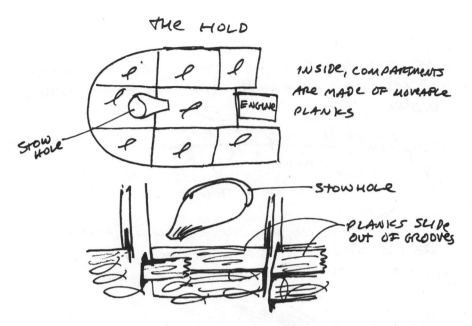

THE HOLD

INSIDE, COMPARTMENTS ARE MADE OF MOVABLE PLANKS

STOW HOLE

ENGINE

STOW HOLE

PLANKS SLIDE OUT OF GROOVES

JOHN MOVES THE PLANKS. HE IS IN UP TO HIS WAIST + STRUGGLING TO EFFECT SOME ARTFUL APPORTIONMENT OF HERRING, BUT THE HERRING SEEMS TO GO RATHER WHERE IT WANTS TO. FIRST WE LIST ONE WAY, THEN THE OTHER.

THERE IS A HANDMADE QUALITY TO THE WHOLE BOAT. THE CONTROL FOR THE REEL IS A ~~ROD~~ ROD ATTACHED AS A LONG FOREARM TO THE ACTUAL CONTROL

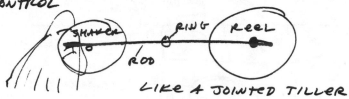

LIKE A JOINTED TILLER

THE NET IS IN DISREPAIR. WHEN IT POPS FROM A SIDE CORD, JOHN PATCHES "WITH A FEW TURNS OF THIS HUGE DARNING NEEDLE

AND ELECTRICAL TAPE.

THE CABIN IS A WARM SANCTUARY <u>W</u> A LITTLE STOVE I'D SAY WAS A WOOD BURNING STOVE EXCEPT I DIDN'T SEE ANY WOOD. IT LOOKS LIKE IT WAS SLAPPED IN <u>W</u> ELECTRICAL TAPE.

FORWARD IN THE TIGHT CABIN ARE OVER-HEAD RACKS OF JARS <u>W</u> SCREWS, BOLTS, NUTS, ASSORTED HARDWARE

'THE HEAD IS THE RAIL,' SAYS PAUL.

AFTER 8 HOURS WE TAKE 10 MINUTES FOR
DOUGHNUTS + COFFEE. ON THE RADIO THERE ARE
MORE CALLS FOR THE DIVER. THE BAY IS ALSO THE
BREEDING GROUND FOR THE GREAT WHITE SHARK,
NOT THIS TIME OF YEAR, THO. JUST HERRING.

THEN WE SEE A BOAT PLOW RIGHT OVER OUR
LAST SET. PAUL + JOHN SHOUT FUTILELY. THE
BOAT NEVER SLOW, NEVER ANSWERS. THEY HOLD THEIR
BREATH. SOMEHOW, THE NET WASN'T TOUCHED. IT'S
OKAY, BUT PAUL REMEMBERS FOR YEARS FISHERMEN
WHO HAVE HIT HIS SETS.

A HARBOR SEAL PATROLS THE SET.
NOT MUCH PAUL CAN DO ABOUT THAT.

THE HERRING ARE COMING BACK, JOHN SAYS. ALSO SARDINE, ADDS PAUL. THESE TWO ARE REAL FISHERMEN.

THE HERRING, UNTIL IT'S READY TO SPAWN, IS ALMOST TRANSLUCENT. IN THAT STATE IT'S CALLED 'GREEN!' IT'S USELESS. BUT LOOK AT THIS! JOHN PICKS UP A FISH + PRESSES HIS THUMB INTO THE BELLY + THE ROE OOZES OUT, PALE YELLOW EGGS

PAUL BREAKS THE FISH OPEN AS IF HE WERE SNAPPING CORNCOBS. THAT'S THE EXPRESSION THE BUYERS WILL USE. THEY 'BREAK' THEM.

FINALLY, AFTER 5½ TONS OF HERRING, HERRING THAT PAUL HAS TRACKED + TRAPPED, THAT JOHN HAS REELED IN, THAT JOHN + I HAVE SQUEEZED THRU THAT TINY HOLE INTO THE HOLD, WE PULL INTO THE DOCK TO UNLOAD. A METAL VACUUM HOSE A FOOT ACROSS IS LOWERED THROUGH THE OPEN HATCH TO JOHN, WHO SUCKS THEM UP, EVERY SINGLE ONE. THE FISH FLY UP TO BE DROPPED ON A

CONVEYOR BELT THAT RUNS RIGHT TO WAITING
TRUCKS. PAUL ASKS JOHN + ME TO COME UP FOR
SOME COFFEE + BRANDY. IT'S 5:30 AM. PAUL
WANTS TO GO OUT AGAIN + CATCH THE DAWN
RUN. ~~NO~~ HE'S A MANIAC WHO HAS BEEN
PROVED RIGHT. NOT ME, I'M GOING HOME.

I DO TAKE A COFFEE + BRANDY FOR THE
DRIVE. THE BUYER'S REP IS IN THE TRAILER,
A YOUNG AMERICAN-JAPANESE w A DENIM
JACKET, BASEBALL CAP, WISPY MUSTACHE.

'15%,' PAUL BEAMS. I'VE BEEN GOOD LUCK.

BEFORE I GET TO THE CAR, I TAKE OFF
SLICKER, SWEAT SHIRT, BOOTS EVEN MY PANTS
BECAUSE I REALLY SMELL.

GARY SNYDER

I've kept a journal of sorts since I was seventeen. It has existed in various formats, some handwritten, some typed, but the forty-five or so volumes are still together, and I can pull any one of them out at any time. I arrived at the basic principles early on: no need to write anything unless you feel like it, anything can go in, no special literary pretension, and no obligation to "make use" of any of it. So they are personal working journals that have proved to be of great use. They are the source of the first drafts of many poems. Nonetheless my notes have run far ahead of my practice of writing, and there is much rich-looking stuff that I have not re-read, let alone copied or edited, lurking back in there.

The journals are not my only record-keeping strategy. I have topical notebooks, topical folders in letter-files, an ancient 3-by-5 card system, and a hard disk. And best, deep memory, where things can be seen, tasted, and touched.

These notes are from a ramble in the central Australian desert with Japanese poet Nanao Sakaki and tracker John Stokes during early October of 1981.

A bit of the entry for 14 October found its way almost verbatim into "Uluru Wild Fig Song," and you will recognize other moments, for example, from 15 October, "trash blowing against fences," as well.

Gary Snyder lives in Nevada City, CA. He is the Pulitzer Prize-winning author of Turtle Island *(New Directions) and a Guggenheim Fellow. His most recent book is* No Nature *(Pantheon).*

8 Oct 1981   Thursday   Alice Springs

— "spangled perch" survives in dry creek
beds between rains — for months —
papunya —

Bill Marshall Stoneking
    (has had some disagreement w/)
Andrew Crocker —
            (Tula Artists = pap.
artists association.
v. book : ... dreaming .. "sandman
            reproductions.
& Art of the Western Desert

artists — Billy Stockman

Eric Maddern   (Madron)
% Araluen Arts and Cultural Trust,
P.O. Box 3057
Alice Springs,
N.T.   5750
Australia
                        Bill Davis
                        his partner.

they've been doing programs in settlements
        singing etc for the kids —

→ Tricia telling me abt govt
has a huge city limits — to make
sure aboriginal land claims won't a
too close — and then enforces a subur
ban style building code across the
whole thing.

　　— shade shelter, plus a lockable
safe storage area — the ideal basic
outback housing. And perhaps a
house w/ firepit, a story of one
such that had been built ____

____? But on complaint of
city ab. types was destroyed. "you
should get the same as the white
man" --

　　use wire mesh for, ramada
overhead, also sides if taking a
climbing plant up it --
wood lattice sides —

or

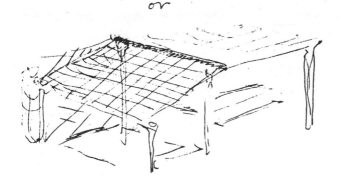

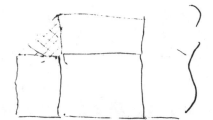

) i.e. check out
ideas for ramada
landscaping

—Alice springs 2000 M.   rain @ 10"—

Michael Last ~~says~~ pitjantjara means "those
who come ~ are coming."

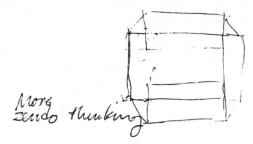

More
zendo thinking

Michael Last — Wheelbarrows of grapes
at Ernabella. A bore @ 600 mm
and 2' deep near a fruit tree (citrus)
filled w/ manure and compost.

—

Digging sticks.
Soak, cure manzanita in the ground
a summer.

8 B continued,

✻ from Hetzel & Firth, paper by R.A Perry,
p. 73, "the 5 landscapes of central
Australia" –

    Hills / Foothills, piedmont plains &
floodplains / lateritic plains /
spinifex sand plains / salt lakes.

Hills

Foothills

laterite

spinifex   salt
     pan

✱ Latz was
one I met at
Wafer's

     Peter
p. 84 Latz ✱ & Griffin, "the concept of
developing an agriculture suitable for the
outstation groups that incorporates at
least some of the knowledge and resources
of the traditional lifestyles has received
little attention."

                  e
                Parenti

9 B. Friday,   Alice Springs
    continuing --
Michael Last also is in Hetzel & Firth.
  – Thermal mass cement block walls
for tomatoes
  – apples into low spots for cold?
  – wire rolls because cheap to
buy and multi-purpose

— The outstation movement — &
Australian gov't paternalism:
— seat belts, bars at 10 pm, compulsory
vote; U.S. base information with held
here that's public info in US. ··

world indigenes are planetary
citizens··

(Land Rights — Outstation — self-sufficiency
— alternative technology
— religion

all connected. For aboriginals

Religion: is self-transcending window
somewhere in there?

Buddhism, the 4 vows, — after centuries
of witnessing invasion, warfare, rapine.

Papua New Guinea — families couldn't
kill or eat their own pet pigs.

yesterday — Nanao and I insist on
taking the day off to be quiet &
catch up — so John and Noreen
go out together in the desert.
— A good long day of organizing &
writing notes — and at 10.30 p
they come back, with a 3 foot

9 B cont.

long stiff brown-dusty cooked
perenti lizard) and a similar
rabbit. We break (?) off the
long tail and peel strips of de-
licious white meat out of it.
Noreen says — don't eat too much,
it's so rich you can get sick
of it.

Centers,
Tracks between,
Tracks that
                cross.

Ayers rock — blacks
        push you right up in the air —
        turn you red —
make your head painted inside
            〰 o r 〰
        sit down in the sand,
                skin to the ground.
roll a hard wild fig on the tongue,
circles, streaks, & lines
                painted in the mind.

(sent to Killigrew)

—yesterday's story of hunting retold over lunch at Noreen's —

4 wheel Toyota bumping and chasing — a kangaroo that got away —

later John shoots the Perenti' and has to also jump out of the truck and pick it up, dash it on a tree.

they start cooking after dark — come home, hands black w/ ash.

READING AT ARALUEN LAWN

// Erik Beech
Neal Murray
poets

Nosepeg

} 3 Papunya
Pintubi singers

Singing a cycle — that would take you clear to Darwin; after an hour they stopped — had gotten to Tenant Creek. A song at each stop. Like Kudachi of Okinawa; like Mohave song-cycles + epic.

— A Queer reading — never took off;
I was feeling low w/ heavy sinus
and bad throat
and then scolded audience for clapping, which I never do—got too
heavy w/ reading "this Tokyo"
and never got it quite light again

COLD started yesterday w/ odd. sinus
went into total clog and sore
throat, heavy mucus & cough.
Air conditioning or pollen.

Kate Jones, of the S. N.T. arts
Council.

———

PM visit to YIPIRIYA school — a
non-recognized Arunta culture
bi-lingual project funded right
now by World Council of Churches
president is Arunta, Eli Rubuntja
—POB 2363 Alice Springs N.T.
Jan, Carol — 目
    Jean Bell — who taped my talk

211

at J.A.D. — works here — and has transcript of that talk, which I clean up — for possible use in a newsletter.

10X81 Alice springs > pupunya

Yirara College all day Saturday Open house — open school — day —

still, bare-breasted painted women do come out and sing, and dance, in the schoolyard.
a digger-stick dance — dancing, looking, probing the ground —

Journey song cycles >
Quest / winter & outer pilgrimage

women dancing, you can hear their breasts flap on their bellies.

A novel about linguistics; dying languages --

11 X 81   Papunya

(Timothy White on Bob
Marley in July '81 Rolling Stone.)
Neal Murray's portable government
house.

Babylon.   = the Metropole
Zion . the Pure Land.
(Alas that it had to be stolen from
others.)

A bed outside on the ground w/
little ants.

...

)" In the western desert
200 miles from Alice Springs
             pintubi, walbiri, country
the streetlights are on all night
the generator rumble is every-
           where.
   outside too bright
   inside too plastic
what sort of people could come
     all this way
And have no place to be
     when they get there. ''

#

Zion — not by force;
the contradictions > chosen people
become the Master Race -- As, Middle
East.

Redemption Songs,
redeem — Get it out of pawn.
Get it back.

Noreen's story of women's refuge
in Alice Springs run by radical lesbians
and the runaway black girl.

Blueing off the barrel, varnish
off the stock, a 12 GA shotgun leans
against the door. Tutinua comes
in, safe, Billy embraces him,

All, South to the foot of the
mountains — for a swim in
a small pond formed by a dam
in a canyon,
Noon — leave for Ilpili.
Neal Murray, Nosepeg,
Green Narband
Tutamu, Razza white teacher lady
from Melbourne, Billy Marshal,
Jimmy Junguri -
bandana

14 ⊟ Wed Papunya ~ Alice

,teki case 83.

Yun-men sd: the Dream-time
and this telephone pole merge. what
level of mental activity is this?" He
answered for himself: "on South
Mountain ~~clouds~~ gather, on North
Mountain rain falls."

the tracks of bulldozers & graders.

Sit on the red sand ground
                with a dog –
breeze blowing, full moon,
   women singing over there
   Old men clapping sticks &
            singing here,
drink black tea.

Bulldozer Dreaming.
("Northern Territory Tidy Towns"
                    movement)

15 ~~H~~   Thursday, Alice Springs.
                → Melbourne

Yesterday —
~~stiff~~ wind - far dust - haze blowing
close ~~to~~ the ground -
    we do ½ hour at the school
~~just before~~ morning break, Nanao
& John drumming — me still without voice do the ~~bigigi~~.
    blonde haired black-skinned   little beauty
dress coming off — untied from behind,
girls mischief on girls, it flies
open, she's completely naked under,
with breasts like mulga mushrooms —
And one boy of 7 or 8 without clothes
in class —

       — trash blowing against the fences.

— people who are waiting to make
       their move, watching what
       this new world, new fellows are —

Two things of great focus: initiation
    & leading thru puberty, and sex.
~~sex~~ and the sacred. } prepared for
                              love-making
{ the fun of love-making
        the rules of love-making   "in the
       The network of kin   vagina
                                    shade"

Kangaroo, wallaby droppings in
near to the waterhole.

A baby kangaroo hairless w/ eyes
closed, taken from its mothers pouch —

—

the early morning bird at toddy's cabins
is —

4 nites.

one more day wandering streets of
Alice, lunch w/ Vicki Nungala &
Nanao, visit w/ Jim Wafer and
a lift to the airport from him;
→ Melbourne.

calligraphy of sand ridges on the
wide ground.

end of Central desert.

\#

GERALD VIZENOR

*T*hese notes are memorial trash and obscure associations with other ideas that came to light for an editorial essay on reservation casinos.

Some of these notions are an innermost summons to the near silence on the road; otherwise, at a distance, these could be the wild words in a vulnerable rubblework. Closer, some notes arise from books and television.

I remember, for instance, reading *The Culture of Contentment* by John Kenneth Galbraith, *The Power of Images* by David Freedberg, and *Society Against the State* by Pierre Clastres at the time these notes were made.

I listed a few page numbers and marked this thought in *The Power of Images:* "We have been fortified by generations of theorists in the view that the wonder and illusions of representation is exactly the opposite of what it has always been supposed to be. Representation is miraculous because it is something other than what it represents." I noted that images cannot be denied representation, and later wrote that the image of the tribes is a miraculous representation.

Cursive notes, on the other hand, could be vaporous in at least two senses: The ideas that are published would disown their incredulous origins, and the rush of notes is seldom readable in the end. I learned twenty years ago, as a reporter for the *Minneapolis Tribune,* that my notes were unstable, impermanent— the unbroken legibility lasted no more than three or four hours.

I hold notes as cues to my ideas and then write in longhand before turning to the weak and unstable shadows of edited sentences on a computer monitor. My obscure notes, at last, are better moored on memorial trash than in monitorial transvaluations.

Gerald Vizenor teaches Native American literature at the University of California, Berkeley. Wesleyan University Press published his most recent novel, The Heirs of Columbus.

... founded on
... malevolence, murder,
deception, of ~~the~~
Tribal cultures.

The tribes are rich with
myths and stories of gamblers,
the ~~figures~~ figurations of
chance and contradiction.

Faustian
bargain
with evil
gambler

The tribes have
never failed to
imagine the
(cosmos would)
and in this
manner the
absurd is
even more absurd

US founded on malevolence, murder, deception of tribal cultures.

The tribes are rich with myths and stories of gamblers, the figurations of chance and contradiction.

Faustian bargain with evil gambler.

The tribes have never failed to imagine the (<u>cosmos</u> world) and in this manner the absurd is even more absurd.

UNIVERSITY OF CALIFORNIA, SANTA CRUZ

BERKELEY • DAVIS • IRVINE • LOS ANGELES • RIVERSIDE • SAN DIEGO • SAN FRANCISCO   SANTA BARBARA • SANTA CRUZ

BENJAMIN F. PORTER COLLEGE   SANTA CRUZ, CALIFORNIA 95064

Columbus idiosyncratic
and we still bow
to his fame
Pitched as menace, to
the dialectics of
politicians, pastors,
philosophers, and
poets.
Columbus landed
in ~~Washington~~
the White House in
Wash.

p 317
is the gaze
possession?

"the long gaze"
fetishizes
If Columbus had been
a woman we might
better understand the
erotic signification of the
male gaze. — p 318
but these are not female bodies
resurrections of Columbus

images cannot be denied
representation 438

Among colonialist discourses

banal

This is about certain images
and the power of names;
the images, ~~and~~ names,
and metaphors that
structure ~~[illegible]~~
~~[illegible]~~
~~[illegible]~~
~~language~~.

a common and
~~dominant~~ neocolonial
realities. This is ~~not~~
~~[illegible]~~
~~lamentation for~~
an invitation to
overturn a more
~~[illegible]~~ and salutation,
rather than ~~so~~
a ~~liberal~~ romantic lamentation
of an anachronistic
creation of cultural avarice
and discoveries

Columbus idiosyncratic and we still dance to his tune

Pitched as increase to the dialectics of political parties, philosophies, and policies.

Columbus landed in the White House in Wash.

p 317

is the gaze possession?

"the long gaze" fetishizes

if Columbus had been a woman we might better understand the erotic signification of the male gaze. —p 318

but this is not female bodies resurrections of Columbus images cannot be denied representation 438

This is about certain images and the power of names, the images, names and metaphors that structure common and neocolonial realities. This is an invitation to overturn a mere name and salutation, rather than a romantic lamentation of an anachronistic victim of cultural avarice and discoveries

however, the liberation of reason
was a denial; the consumers
lost their wisdom and the
tribes were denied chance
and humor — liberation for
one was a categorical
imperative for the other

How do we hold our
experience — who control
memories?

How is it possible, given
the demands and
distractions of survivance,
that the tribes were
more noble, more
spiritual, more
profound in their
sense of responsibility
for communities; are
we to believe that
technologies and
education are enemies
of tribal ecstasies?
If the burdens of
survivance in the
past revealed the
paradise in our
soul then we
seek our presence
on the streets;
then we must
abandon tech, autos
and television, and
seek our visions in
the ruins of a
chem civilization

the present is reexperation,
~~a performance~~
~~spiritual existentialism is~~
a performance, and the
past is remembered in
stories, performance an
~~existentialism~~ that
is established in the
written word. memories
are stories not personal
~~traditions~~; the past that
~~separated and~~ expressed by religion
and ideologies ~~to~~

The separation and revision
of personal memories ~~by~~
are traditions. The tropes
to power ~~in the tribal~~
are traditions as ~~methods~~
theories are the sources of
power in neocolonial
social sciences. Traditions
and tropes to power in
any culture are ~~most~~
~~a~~ reductive denials of
liberation.

The hallucinogenic
substances of denial;
~~The chemical of~~
treasures of a chemical
civilization are
discovered to overcome
the lonesome denial
of tragic wisdom.

The rational denial of tragic
wisdom as unproductive
and a weakness to power
capitalism
colonialism
how long to read Bergi over
or control

However, the liberation of reason was a denial; the consumers lost their wisdom and the tribes were denied chance and humor—liberation for one was a categorical imperative for the other

How do we hold our experience—who controls memories?

How is it possible, given the demands and distractions of survivance, that the tribes were more noble, more spiritual, more profound in their sense of responsibilities for communities; are we to believe that technologies and education are enemies of tribal ecstasies? If the burdens of survivance in the past revealed the paradise in our soul then we seek our presence in the streets; then we must abandon tech, autos and television, and seek our vision in the ruins of a chem civilization

the present is respiration, and the past is remembered in stories, of performance and of spiritual existentialism that is established in the written word. Tribal memories are stories not traditions. The personal past that is separated and revised by religion and ideologies

The separation and revision of personal memories are traditions. The tropes to power are traditions as theories are the sources of power in neocolonial social sciences. Traditions and tropes to power in any culture are denials of liberation.

The hallucinogenic substances of denial; the treasures of a chemical civilization are discovered to overcome the lonesome denial of tragic wisdom.

The rational denial of tragic wisdom as unproductive and a weakness to power capitalism, colonialism
how long to resist Bingo or control

The Tribe died or
translation; at last (?)
— the breath of foreign
was buried on the
page.
The Tribes died became
they resisted
change and became
the — Friends

To close or mangled over
a traitor's as to clear
domination over liberation;
the Friends' liberate
the _____ said in
stars and language
games but to ____
games on the line
mangle as he
of an mangled as he
not to pretend
information. Neither
the traitors nor
the mangled art
the evangelist but
representation but
the listener determines
the presence (
resignation, we know)
or liberation.

The tribes died in translation; at last, the breath of savagism was buried on the page.

The tribes died because they resisted change and became the—tourists.

To choose an evangelist over a trickster is to choose domination over liberation; the trickster liberates the spirit in stories and language games, but to pursue the line of an evangelist is to pretend victimization. Neither the trickster nor the evangelist are representation, but the listeners determine the presence of resignation, evilness, or liberation.

colonial and imperial in OK
the class arrogance, however, ~~tone~~
is a slipstream and comes
closer to tragic erosion than
consciousness and cultural power.
There are too many endowed
chairs and no bookstores
worth remembering on or
near the campus. The
bedrooms
campus ~~so dead~~ commonwealth chances
are dead, but the Gardens
like the ~~use bleached~~. Arise and
culture are
parmes proud cloving from a
catalogue. that are pure ardent

~~deloderates~~
defreent declaration
To downward;
patriotism and

Colonial and imperial in OK [Oklahoma]

The class arrogance, however, is a slipstream and comes closer to tragic ironies than consciousness and cultural power.

There are too many endowed chairs and no bookstores worth remembering on or near the campus. The campus communities are dead bedrooms but the chemical gardens like the culture are defiant declarations of patriotism and dominance; Wise and proud blooms that are ordered from a catalogue.

The individual in the communal — individualism in itself is not the problem — but underlying isolation and compulsion is — separation as hierarchy is known.

The natural world is dangerous. The communal ceremonies are not enough — survival depends upon the individual vision. — The shaman in service to communities.

How else would those who are visited with uncommon and ecstatic visions to endure. Problem is too many uncommon people in community shift the burden of communal responsibility to possessions association which become elitist and exclusive compulsive — come together symbiotically as ball teams — sports etc

The individual in the communal—individualism in itself is not the problem—but individual isolation and competition is—separation as hierarchy is trouble.

The natural world is dangerous. The communal ceremonies are not enough—survivance depends upon the individual vision—the shaman in service to communities.

How else would those who are visited with uncommon and ecstatic visions to endure. Problem is, too many unknown people in communities shift the burdens of communal responsibilities to professional associations which become elitist and exclusive, competitive—come together symbolically as ball teams—sports etc

Bingo, the death g tribal dream; bingo, the
ruin g tribal contradictions;
Bingo, the cash g losers cash is
the end g the tribe —

[Standing Bear
Potlach]

Bingo has no music
Bingo is not a tribal
game channel, the game
is our ruin; there is
no music.

The evil gambler created
(introduced bingo or casinos
on the reservation; and
so
once more the tribes
must gamble for their
lives and culture.
To win at bingo is to
lose to the evil gambler

Bingo, the death of tribal dream; bingo, the ruin of tribal contradictions; Bingo, the cash of losers cash is the end of the tribe—

[Standing Bear Potlatch]

Bingo has no music

Bingo is not a tribal chance, the game is our ruin; there is no music.

The evil gambler created (introduced) bingo or casinos on the reservation; once more the tribes must gamble for their lives and culture. To win at bingo is to lose to this evil gambler

DAVID RAINS WALLACE

My notebooks are mainly field journals. Sometimes they include drafts, ideas, dreams, conversations, etc. Their main function is to remind me of the details of things I might want to write about later. They're mnemonic devices—if I'm reminded of objective details, subjective experience usually comes back. In contrast, remembering subjective experience doesn't usually recall objective details. Details are essential to the kind of writing I do, although I don't use most of what I record in journals. But I never know what I might want to use.

I generally pack 8½-by-11 spiral notebooks and record things at the end of the day, although I sometimes carry pocket notebooks and record things on the spot, depending on how much precise detail I want. I've occasionally used three sizes—small, medium, and large—but this gets unwieldy, with notebooks falling out of every pocket. I've also used a pocket cassette recorder for conversations. This is more reliable than notebooks, but makes some people nervous, especially scientists. It also has to be transcribed, which I've never bothered to do with written notebooks even though my handwriting is so bad. It has always been bad: when younger, I feared it was a symptom of mental disorder, but I'm not demented yet and it hasn't gotten worse.

These pages are from a journal I kept at a biological station at Volcan Cacao in Costa Rica's Guanacaste National Park in 1988. They were used in writing an essay, "Tapirs' Gourds and Smelly Toads: Life in a Little-Known Rainforest," which was included in *The Nature of Nature,* published by Harcourt Brace. I did a lot of drawing in this journal because I didn't know the names of most of the plants and I knew I wouldn't be able to remember them any other way. At the time, the Volcan Cacao rain forest and cloud forest hadn't been surveyed biologically, and nobody knew much about the plants.

David Rains Wallace lives in Berkeley. His most recent book is The Quetzal and the Macaw: The Story of Costa Rica's National Parks *(Sierra Club Books).*

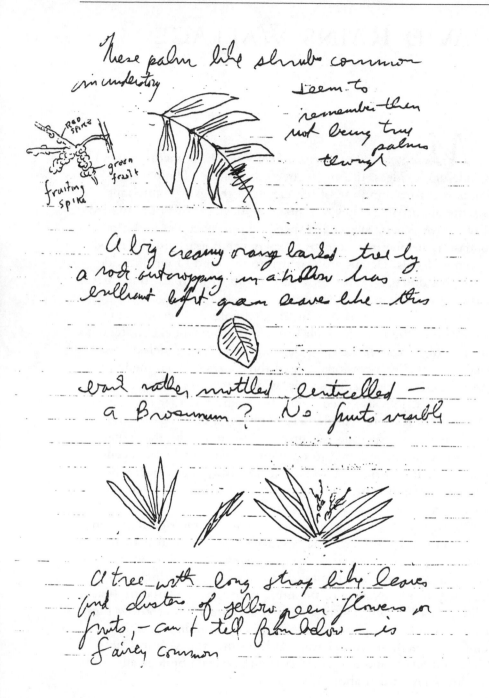

These palm like shrubs common in understory   Seem to remember them not being true palms though

Red Spike
green fruit
fruiting spike

A big creamy orange larked tree by a rock outcropping in a hollow has brilliant bright green leaves like this

Leaf rather mottled lenticelled — a Brosimum? No fruits visible

A tree with long strap like leaves and clusters of yellow green flowers or fruits, — can't tell from below — is fairly common

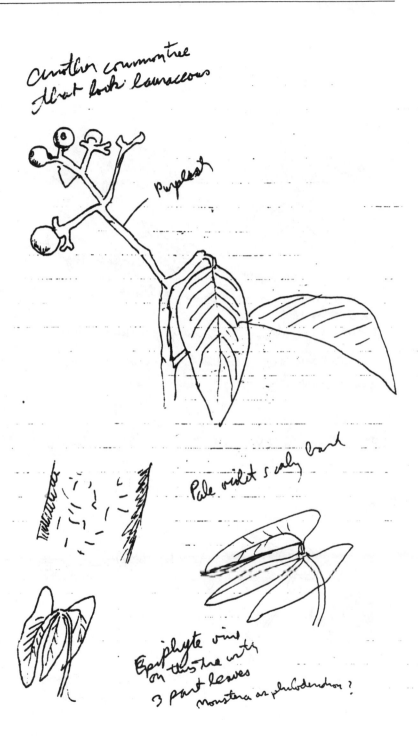

Another common tree
that look lauraceous

Purplest

Pale violet scaly bark

Epiphyte vine
on this tree with
3 part leaves
monstera or philodendron?

Beautiful scarlet lobelia
like small shrub with
glossy green - dark leaves

Protruding stamens

in sunny area
beside trail on
other side of ridge

platform — yellow target

stamens seem
to develop after — inside of flower
lower lip withers — timing for pollination.
— See large green butterfly with small red
spots visit it.

Some trees — have stilt roots instead
of buttresses — wonder why — Not just
Socratea palm (which not here) but
other trees

3 part
fruit

Common
ivy leaved
shrub
Michael collected

5 part
fleshy
flower

Milky sap
Euphorbia?
— I think same genus or family
"Danto" in Canara

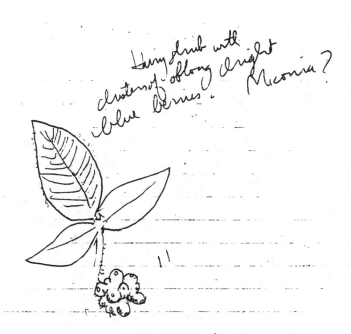

Hairy shrub with clusters of oblong bright blue berries. Miconia?

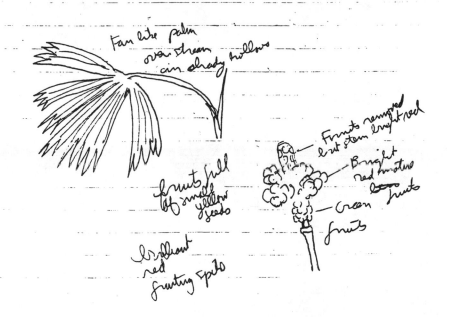

Fan like palm over stream in shady hollow

Fruits full of small yellow seeds

Brilliant red fruiting spike

Fruits removed but stem bright red

Bright red mature fruits

Green fruits

Surprising how many brilliant red ~~things~~ hiding in green. Forest floor littered in many places with small urn shaped red blossoms 

See some masses of red, tubular blossoms in ~~treetops~~ that might be epiphyte flowers, poss above?

Walking back, see big greenish ~~brown~~ sweet potato like fruits on ground, pieces broken out of them, look ~~and~~ around, finally realize small tree right beside trail has the fruits all up and down its pale, irregular trunk – it's another ~~Jicaro~~ Jicaro de Danta, Parmentiera, but app different species from one Janzen showed me because fruits so different – Some are ~~ex~~ 8–10 inches long like dry cucumbers

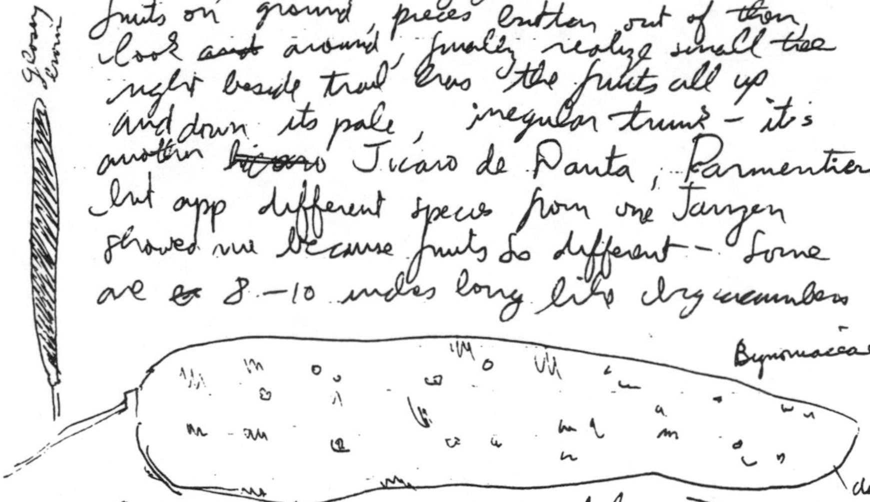

Glossy brown
Bignoniaceae
dark green
like bad potato

flowers and leaves more like Janzen's

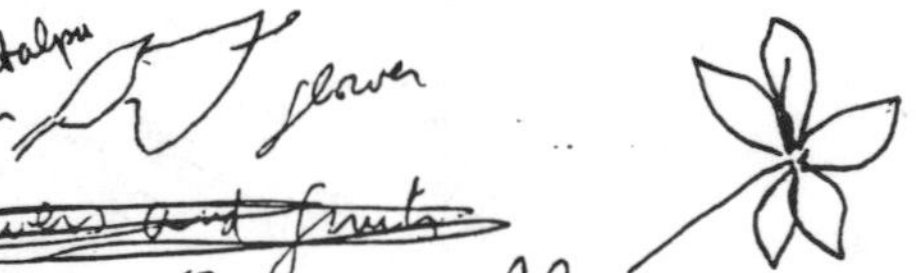

is like catalpa flower
flower
leaf

~~flowers and fruits~~

a flowers all over ground and

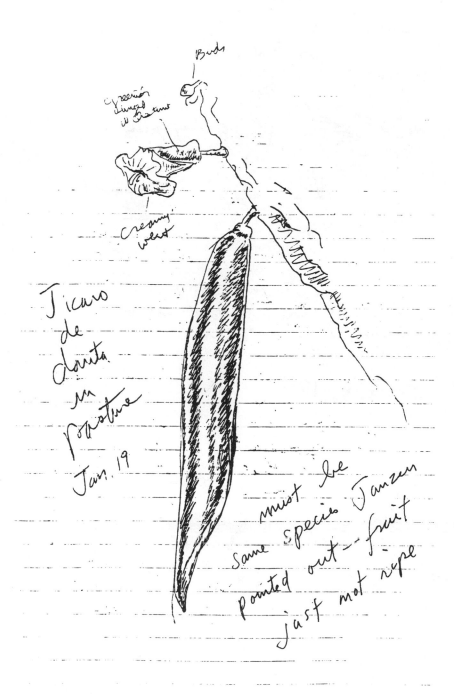

Buds

Greenish
tinged in
the tone

Creamy
white

Jicaro
de
Clorita
in
pasture

Jan. 19

must be
same species Janzen
pointed out -- fruit
just not ripe

Tree in pasture with pinnate
compound leaves

5 opposite sets of
leaflets

glossy green

4 valved
fruits

On top of stream gorge are
many feathery pinnate palms
bending in the wind

inflorescence

Striking solanaceous looking shrub on bottomland

5 parted
flower

beginning
fruit

large bright glossy
red pepper like fruit

opened fruit with leaf

Smallish tree with mottled, sycamore
like bark; opposite, wavy margined
leaves is fairly common. Don't
see fruits.

Go ~~sit~~ & stand in underbrush
along small tributary for awhile.
Completely sunk in green leaves. Unseen
Bird whistles low & melodious
occasionally changing tones — try
imitating it but doesn't come
into sight. Little troop of 4–5
coatis passes, all along pretty much
same path, tails in air, ~~cross~~ noses
to ground, cross creek, disappear.
A bird flies past quite close,
so fast that it is gone again
before I realized it perched on a
branch right before my nose a
second. Too close for me to focus
on it. Then it perches farther
away and I see it's a long
tailed mangrin - blue back clearly
visible. stays long enough for me
to try to get binoculars on it, then
is off at this movement. It was

they are doing the whistling.
Find & press pink ?? stemmed
orchid on way back.
Sun. Jan 17. — Rain in the night
again but clearing by morning; Gets
warmer than will; even been by
noon.

Starting out at 7 ~~come upon small~~,
smell foetid, ~~something~~ musky
odor along lower part of trail —
think some big mammal about.
Then find smaller (2½ in.) purple gray
toad crossing trail. Its skin not
warty, but ridged, like worn leather,
color paler on the ridges.

Notice foetid odor increases
markedly when I disturb it
with a stick - like zoo monkey house.
Makes no try to get away & doesn't
even struggle when I turn it
over with stick. Like playing
possum, which also stinks.

Sudden burst of very loud whistling birdsong
from underbrush. Rich distinct notes going
up & down scale. Lee nothing. Also
clear woodthrush like song, & howler
monkeys further off.

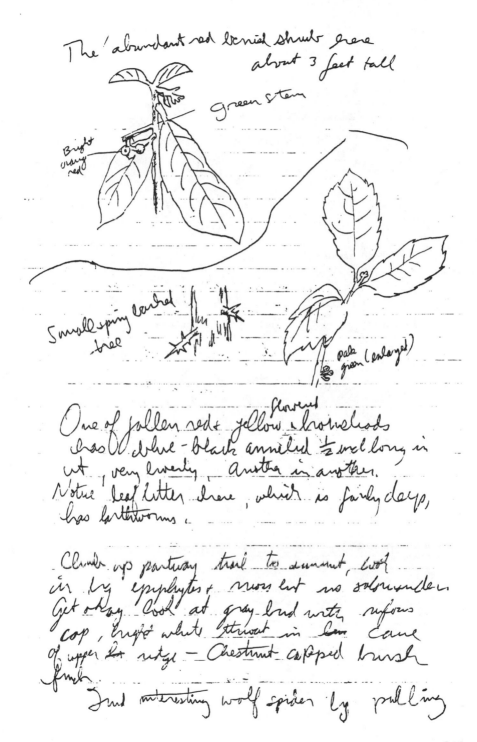

The 'abundant red berried shrub here about 3 feet tall

green stem

Bright orange red

Small spiny leaved tree

pale green (enlarged)

One of fallen red + yellow flowered horseheads has dull blue-black annulid ½ inch long in it, very lovely. Another in another. Notice leaf litter here, which is fairly deep, has earthworms.

Climb up partway trail to summit, look in by epiphytes + moss but no salamanders. Get okay look at gray bird with rufous cap, bright white throat in low cane of upper ridge — Chestnut capped brush finch. Find interesting wolf spider by pulling

thin bark of a tree up there
(small denacoustos) — flattened, about
an inch long — rufous runs around tree
like squirrel.

Back legs
held over abdomen

Which reminds me saw small squirrel
again this morning — scolded me
flirting tail just like chickaree —
seems a little grayer today.

common strap - leave
tree of high ridges —
looks a little like
Drimys but no fruits

Come down from Summit Trail and
proceed down other side of ridge — Encounter
a big black gallinaceous bird on small
tree right by trail — red eyes and feet —
blue skin before beak — otherwise all
black. Stands some time eyeing me
anxiously as I stand still, then hops
to another tree, slightly longer, which

also contains an emerald toucanet,
Toucanet flies off, black bird — hops away
uphill still eyeing me. Not in Peterson,
Black man? Don't see any fruits nearby that would be attracted
cut of toucanet.
All this just uphill from big fruit
jicaro de danta I found yesterday. The
forest here smells oddly like th'
soap they provide in Costa Rican hotels.

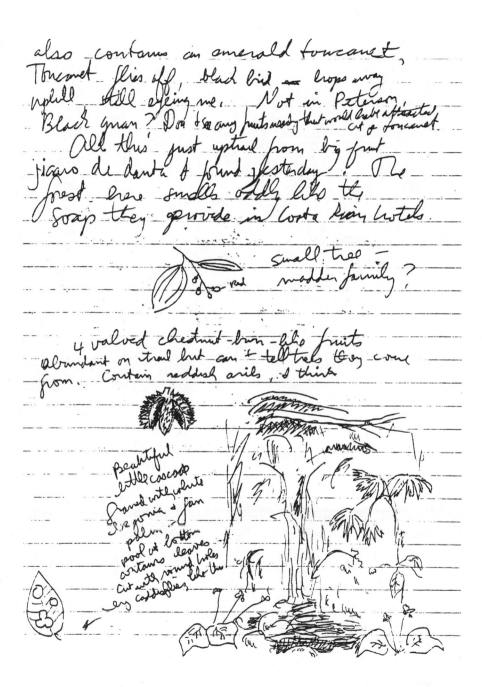

small tree —
madder family?

4 valved chestnut-brown-like fruits
abundant on trail but can't tell trees they come
from. Contain reddish arils, I think

Beautiful
little cascade
framed with white
begonia & fan
palm —
pool at bottom
contains leaves
cut with round holes
eg castroflies, like this

About the Editor

Howard Junker founded *ZYZZYVA,* a quarterly of West Coast writers and artists, in 1985. In 1991 he edited a selection of essays from its pages, *Roots and Branches,* published by Mercury House. Junker has worked as a carpenter, cook, junior high school teacher, and TV producer, and has written for *Art in America, Esquire, The Nation, Newsweek,* and *Rolling Stone* magazines. He lives with his wife and their daughter in San Francisco.